More Praise for
Learning Experience Design Essentials

"Dive into the core principles of learning experience design with Cara's practical, hands-on guide. She walks you through how to craft effective and engaging learning experiences to enable optimal workforce performance."
—**Brandon Carson,** Vice President, Learning and Leadership, Walmart

"With this book, Cara North shows why she's a respected leader in our field. If you're looking for real talk, practical exercises, and actionable advice that will help you create meaningful learning experiences, this is a must-read."
—**Jonathan Hill,** Head of E-Learning, Entain Customer Services

"*Learning Experience Design Essentials* transforms ideas to clear paths for creating real-work experience design programs. It inspires designers to add realism and practicality to their learners' learning."
—**Ray Jimenez,** PhD, Chief Learning Architect, Vignettes Learning, Inc., and Situation Expert

"Cara's book is a fantastic resource for professionals who are new to instructional design or those who have been in the trenches for a while, and I love that she includes 30/60/90-day plans as well as other resource tools as guidance in every chapter! I found myself laughing and shaking my head as I read her spot-on reflections and examples."
—**Debbie Richards,** President, Creative Interactive Ideas

"This changing industry demands so much more now than mere instructional design. Fiercely competent and compassionate, Cara plainly maps out each LXD principle to support what our job has always been: empowering people to succeed at their work."
—**Jonathan Rock,** MBA, Senior GMP Training Specialist, Zoetis

"Learning experience design is one of those phrases that can mean different things depending on whom you ask. Cara North does an outstanding job breaking down LXD in a practical way anyone can execute back on the job."

—**Tim Slade,** Freelance E-Learning Designer, The eLearning Designer's Academy

"Cara North provides much needed clarity around the core capabilities of a learning experience designer and how the role can positively affect change in any organization."

—**Joseph Suarez,** Learning Experience Designer, Suarez Media Production

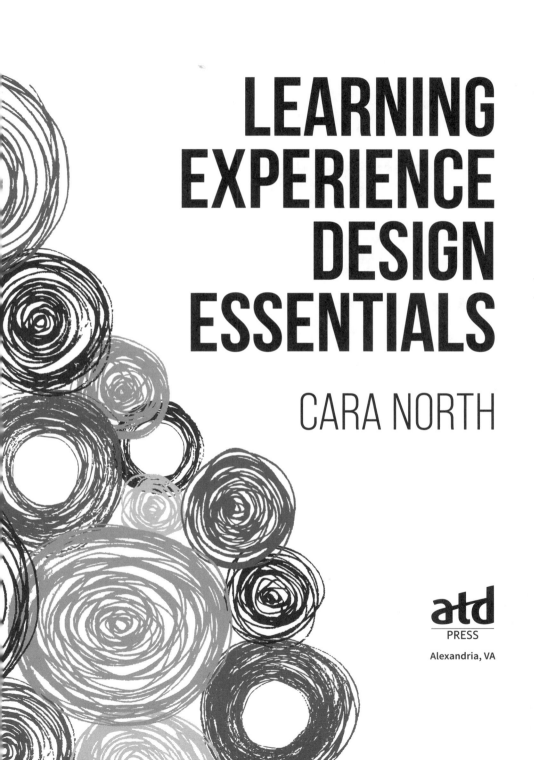

LEARNING EXPERIENCE DESIGN ESSENTIALS

CARA NORTH

atd
PRESS

Alexandria, VA

ATD Press is an internationally renowned source of insightful and practical information on talent development, training, and professional development.

ATD Press
1640 King Street
Alexandria, VA 22314 USA

Ordering information: Books published by ATD Press can be purchased by visiting ATD's website at td.org/books or by calling 800.628.2783 or 703.683.8100.

Library of Congress Control Number: 2023934805

ISBN-10: 1-95394-642-9
ISBN-13: 978-1-953946-42-3
e-ISBN: 978-1-95394-643-0

ATD Press Editorial Staff
Director: Sarah Halgas
Manager: Melissa Jones
Content Manager, Learning and Development: Jes Thompson
Developmental Editors: Jack Harlow and Hannah Sternberg
Production Editor: Katy Wiley Stewts
Text Designer: Shirley E.M. Raybuck
Cover Designer: Brandon Rush

Printed by Color House Graphics, Grand Rapids, MI

To my mother, Carolyn, whose guidance and

wit shaped me into the person I am today.

I love and miss you, Mom.

Contents

Introduction
A Call to Action

It's the news that no one wants to hear: an impromptu meeting with HR appears on your work calendar with no context. Hearing the words "your job has been eliminated," no matter the context, is always difficult. Over the years, this has happened to too many people I care about in the talent development industry.

I joined the talent development field accidentally, but I stayed in it because I love helping and being part of someone's success. That success could be upskilling to a new role; it could be doing your job better; or it could simply be the satisfaction of finding an answer when you need it. The work that we do in learning and development is essentially about being in the people business. People are complex creatures with free will and often have many emotional layers. Regardless of the complexities, I hope we can all agree that the dehumanization many experience when losing their jobs leaves a scar that is difficult to heal.

As I saw this happening across the talent development field, I wanted to do something. So in 2020, I started posting a roundup of open instructional design jobs on LinkedIn to try to help as many folks as possible. What started as a weekly post turned into at least three to four posts a week. This gesture became a habit, and I connected with many people who said that they found their next opportunity through my posts. Along the way, I read many job descriptions, which got me thinking about the evolving roles in instructional design. After reading so many job postings, one thing became clear to me: Instructional design as I knew it had an identity problem.

The "Instructional Designer" Is an Endangered Species

I got my start in the talent development field by doing some training in a call center. It wasn't my primary role, but it was by far the most enjoyable part of my job. Then, when I went to work at Amazon, I had an opportunity to work as an instructional designer; I wasn't the one delivering the content, but I was planning it. Believe it or not, this was before e-learning authoring tools, so I'd storyboard and map the curriculum and build it in the learning management system (LMS). Because this was my formative instructional design work experience, I thought the instructional designer was also the curriculum mapper and the e-learning developer.

It has become rare that job postings looking for an instructional designer seek someone who only designs learning content. Today's job postings want someone who can do everything: needs assessments, storyboarding and curriculum mapping, e-learning development, LMS administration, knowledge management, learning information architecture, assessment and evaluation, and the list goes on. It is no longer enough to be an instructional designer. Those who can't transition and do more, sadly, have been left behind. So, what happened to the OG instructional designer in the workplace? Their role has been adapted by organizations that don't fully understand the value of what instructional designers bring to the talent development team. Further compounding this issue, if you ask 20 instructional designers to provide an instructional design job description, you will get 20 different answers. This is due to the vast differences in how instructional design is operationalized in our organizations.

But my hunch wasn't good enough for me; it fed my curiosity to do academic research on the topic. From the beginning of June 2020 through the end of July 2020, my research colleagues and I collected instructional design job descriptions from a variety of resources including LinkedIn, Indeed, and HigherEdJobs. While it was impossible to collect all titles similar to instructional designer, we did search for other terms—like *LMS curriculum developer* and *corporate learning and development specialist*—and we set the following inclusion criteria (Figure I-1).

Figure I-1. Inclusion Criteria for Job Description Research

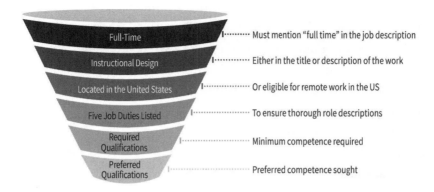

We then coded the job descriptions that fit our inclusion criteria in accordance with the three main capabilities of ATD's Talent Development Capability Model (Figure I-2). We wanted to answer the question, "What can we learn about the requirements of instructional designers from current job descriptions in comparison to the Talent Development Capability Model?"

Figure I-2. The ATD Talent Development Capability Model

My assumption before doing this work was that the instances mentioning parts of the Impacting Organizational Capability (IO), specifically

business insight and performance support, would be through the roof. It wasn't that way at all. Among the three domains within the Talent Development Capability Model, the Developing Professional Capability (DP) had far more mentions than the other two. When analyzing 100 job postings, we found 346 instances of DP, while there were 193 instances of the Building Personal Capability (BP) and only 94 instances of IO (North et al. 2021). I deconstructed these findings because I was truly shocked at the results. I wondered if this was the result of an assumption that some IO skills and capabilities were necessary and inherent to instructional designers, and so didn't need to be spelled out in job descriptions.

The research only increased my curiosity and fueled my quest to understand how we do the work we do. What is the work that instructional designers do? Often, it's building storyboards or mapping curriculum, but, especially in the past few years, I've seen more job descriptions require IDs to also do the work of an e-learning developer. Also, depending on their organizations, IDs may facilitate training sessions virtually or in person. So how many hats should an instructional designer wear, and what does this mean for the future of our work?

Organizations Want More Results on a Quicker Timeline

Talent development functions are often not money makers; they are money takers, and our organizations are aware of this fact. Many companies see the work we do through a lens of risk mitigation.

Imagine you create a training course on how to manufacture a widget. This course is delivered to every widget maker in the factory. Every widget maker completes the training course and passes based on a poorly written multiple-choice test. (Don't worry; we will talk about assessment and evaluation later.) A few weeks later, a widget maker makes a mistake on the job, damaging the equipment used to manufacture the widget. The organization does a root-cause analysis and determines that because the training course covered the relevant process, the widget maker should be terminated. The widget maker sues, saying they were not trained appropriately to make the widget, and is seeking back pay and damages. Meanwhile, you are now in the hot seat for your training course. Why did you build it this way? Is it legally defensible in a court of law?

While scary, this example is based on a real situation (although in a different industry). It was a mess for all parties involved. For the widget maker, they felt like they were set up to fail. Why were they expected to be perfect on the job when their only training was a course that everyone went through once? They didn't have an opportunity to ask questions or a safe environment to practice in. For the organization, a lot of money was paid to the talent development department via salaries, learning technologies, and professional development. If the department can't protect the business in situations like this, what good is it? For you, who created the training course, maybe you were set up to fail by a pushy subject matter expert (SME), a tight timeline, and nothing more than a content dump of PowerPoint slides to use as the basis of the course.

I like to say that I'm not in the underwear business, so I don't want learning experiences to only be used to cover the bums of the organization. Are we now expected to be legal experts who can provide our organizations with legally defensible learning experiences? If this is something you haven't thought about yet, you likely will at some point during your career. Many organizations use the learning experiences we create as punitive compliance orders instead of as support functions to employees. I'm not going to sugarcoat it; your mileage may vary depending on where your department sits in the organization, your leadership, the composition of the talent development team, and the size and geographic footprint of the company.

I encourage you to put this in your skillet and let it simmer so the message is very clear: Our organizations want better results, yet they often dictate resources (people and money) without allowing for requests from us.

What Is Learning Experience Design (LXD)?

To this point, I've discussed instructional design. You may be reading this wondering why the title of this book is *Learning Experience Design Essentials*. So, what is the difference? To me, *learning experience design (LXD)* is the combination of content and context to enable human performance—and that's what elevates LXD. That's what the widget maker situation described in the previous section actually needed.

Content is a combination of the information, images, and media that help provide enough knowledge to enable someone to execute a task. Traditional instructional design focuses on the content but often misses the mark on one critical piece: the human connection. How does someone relate to or engage with the learning experience? My PhD advisor, Kui Xie, a scholar in student motivation and engagement, published some research on the topic of learning engagement that came up with three constructs: behavioral engagement, cognitive engagement, and emotional engagement (Xie, Heddy, and Greene 2019). I've embraced these constructs because if you search for an answer to the question "What is learner engagement?" you'd get so many responses. These three constructs of engagement, as outlined in Table I-1, make sense when crafting learning experiences.

Table I-1. Constructs of Engagement

Behavioral	Cognitive	Emotional
What are they doing?	How are they being challenged?	How does it make them feel?

Too often, the instructional design approach doesn't consider the emotional engagement construct. While some IDs have embraced techniques such as empathy mapping and design thinking, too often the focus is only on the content in the learning experience. Going back to the point of the work that we do to help empower people to do their jobs better and move up in their careers, can we truly do that without a level of engagement and emotional connection? That's where context comes in.

Context comprises everything going on while learners attempt to apply content to the job. One of my favorite quotes from Michael Allen (2020) is "when it's time to perform that is not the time to practice." How often are there gaps in content from someone taking a traditional e-learning course on a topic but not being able to apply it for months? Worse is when they are forced into a one-and-done system, which is how many learning technologies share content. If someone wants a refresh later, they often have to go back through the e-learning course in its entirety. LXD embraces the idea that people need practice and resources to enable performance. This isn't a new concept—Judith Hale and other human performance pioneers have beat this drum for years—but I think that as we pivoted from instructor-led training to e-learning, so much emphasis was put on the aesthetics that the content and ultimately the human experience got lost. So much of instructional design is cognitive, meaning it focuses on what someone should know about a topic. Even the term *instructional design*, emphasis on instructional, implies being told what to do, almost as if there is an authoritative figure pointing a finger at you. While this may work in some situations, I argue that the modern workplace is far more nuanced and needs an approach that isn't one-size-fits-all. In fact, I've been guilty of this myself, but I'd often rather work than take a required e-learning course that is created in a punitive way with locked navigation, quiz questions that can be easily guessed, and so much content I can't remember what happened three slides ago. Context takes into consideration the work environment, the type of person who is in the environment, and the challenges in execution. Context matters and is missing in some instructional design approaches.

I fear that if L&D doesn't change across the board to focus on content and context (learning experience design) over shiny deliverables, we will be written off as transactional. Allow me to give an example to illustrate this point.

I had the honor of speaking to M. David Merrill and had the opportunity to ask him a question: What is the relationship between learning technologies and instructional design? He crafted a beautiful analogy of a semitruck and cargo. According to Merrill, the impact of a learning experience is the cargo, and the learning technology that delivers it is like a semitruck (as depicted in Figure I-3). When we focus so much on the learning technology and shy away from the learning experience design, we are missing the point. The semitruck can have all the bells and whistles, but if the content is broken or the context isn't incorporated, it's like the cargo showing up damaged and unusable. It doesn't matter that the semitruck is fancy if the cargo isn't what you needed. How often is the focal point on what a learning authoring tool can do or what features an LMS has instead of on the content and how it will be used in context? L&D becomes transactional instead of meaningful when the focus is delivering shiny e-learning modules (big fancy trucks) instead of effective learning experiences (usable cargo).

Figure I-3. Semitruck and Cargo Metaphor From M. David Merrill

What to Expect in This Book

Through sharing my experience, I hope to provide you with value, whether you are just getting started on your LXD journey or wanting to try new things in your work. I've had an eclectic work background, starting in a call center and then working at Amazon before moving into higher education, learning leadership, and finally to full-time consulting. These experiences have shaped me into the talent development professional I am today. I've also been fortunate enough to be formally educated in learning theory and science. I enjoy keeping a foot in the higher education space as an adjunct professor at Boise State University and as a reader of learning research; I even do my own academic research.

Also, to be transparent, I have made a lot of mistakes! While I think that failure is a critical part of the learning process, I argue we should make it cool to fail in our learning experiences as long as we're in a safe environment to do so. This book will be full of stories and mistakes I've made along the way. This certainly doesn't mean I'm perfect now or that I ever will be, but I hope that you are able to relate to my experiences and consider if you've had similar situations. I hope my stories spark you to reflect on how you would have done things differently.

This book is for folks new to instructional design and those looking to elevate their skills and strategy. If you don't fit these roles, I still hope it can add value to your toolkit. I want to help you transform learning experiences by embracing the idea that learning is a process, not a onetime event. This book also discusses what it takes to lead to results, whether in a corporate, higher education, or consulting setting. Its contents will help you transition away from knowledge dumps to focus on the content and context of how people will be experiencing learning events. This book will also carefully tie the relationship of learning technologies to content development, and it will consider this topic from a less prescriptive approach, which will give you questions to ponder as you make choices. There is no one-size-fits-all approach.

From an actionable standpoint, use this book as a resource and work through the activities. One of the main activities will be crafting a 30/60/90-day plan to apply various concepts throughout. This can be done at a conceptual or summative level (or both). Chapters will include sample 30/60/90 plans, but the best action plans are those written by you because you know more about your individual situation. The provided 30/60/90 plans will be very high level, and I encourage you to consider them as guidance only. Additionally, we explore various questions throughout this book that should make you think hard about why you do what you do when it comes to creating learning experiences. These are meant for you to reflect on your own practices, deconstruct previous work, and consider how to transform it to an LXD approach. Finally, this book will share one of my favorite exercises that I learned a long time ago but still get utility from: the humble task analysis. Task analyses provide so much value; I'll share how a task analysis can help answer the questions of both content and context when creating learning experiences.

In the next chapter, and throughout this book, I want to make an argument for moving away from the content-driven approach that has plagued instructional design for decades and pivoting to a holistic approach that embraces both the content and the context. This approach, learning experience design, is the foundation of this book, and I hope to give you the tools and approaches that will help you design learning experiences with impact, whether you are a corporate, higher education, or consultant practitioner. Let's get started!

Chapter 1

What Is Learning Experience Design (LXD)?

In this chapter, we will explore:

◉ How learning experience design is operationalized

◉ Some capabilities of learning experience design

In the introduction, I outlined how my curiosity around job descriptions led me down the path to exploring learning experience design (LXD), which I anchored in engagement constructs. There has been an interest from many professionals across the broader learning and development field in exploring how user experience and instructional design overlap. Is that what learning experience design is?

I first heard the term *learning experience design* in 2016 while I was a staff member and graduate student at The Ohio State University. The first time I heard it, I wondered how it differed from *instructional design*. Then, in 2017, I became a founding member of the learning experience design research group at Ohio State, which explored the intersection of user experience and learning experiences. My friend and colleague, Ceren Korkmaz, took it a step further by researching and working in industrial design. Through a mini experiment, we lectured a group of industrial design students about learning experience design to see how they could apply their design expertise to building learning experiences. To say I was blown away with the final products would be an understatement.

Their attention to user research as well as their consideration of multiple types of end products inspired me to dig deeper. At the time, I was a higher education instructional designer, an independent consultant, and a graduate student. The summer after that course, I landed a contract leading soft skills training courses with a large music industry client. I remember trying to dive into some more research around the user experience, but I was completely shot down and told to just crank out an e-learning module, take my money, and go. There had to be a better way.

Content and Context

So, is learning experience design the combination of what I call the OG instructional designer (or someone who does front-end analysis and curriculum development) and the e-learning developer? Some people would say yes. Part of the problem is that there isn't uniformity from organization to organization in how companies define the learning experience designer job. A good learning experience, which encompasses the entire campaign and not just a training session, also varies. Some organizations welcome the idea of learning experiences, while others refuse to change. To me, learning experience design is a holistic lens through which I see the way learning experiences are developed. It's not a "spray and pray" interaction; rather, it considers the intention of the content and how it will be used in the organization to design the best experience for that use. It's about not thinking that one learning experience equates mastery, but it's about considering how the content can be delivered in a way that gives users many opportunities to recall and apply the content while they perform their jobs. It's not assuming that people will be engaged via a drag-and-drop interaction; it's the knowledge, as Thiagi has said, that "engagement is in the mind, not the mouse."

What does this look like in the real world? Let's look at an example from my time as a training manager: An email came to me from a value stream manager who had made a PowerPoint presentation about preventing defects with a product our organization manufactured. The email stated that the manager would like us to upload the PowerPoint deck and assign it to everyone in the department for awareness. The organization was increasing the yield of this particular product, which was complicated to manufacture due to a long cycle time. The PowerPoint presentation included several pictures of defects but no information about potential causes, no information on safeguards for prevention, and no information on what to do if a defect was detected. A team member reached out to the manager to set up a meeting to discuss the content further. When she did, it was like opening Pandora's box. She learned so much more about the department and their constraints—from staffing all the way to the lighting in the department's area, which could make it difficult for employees to see the defects. She asked what metrics the department was being held accountable for and found that a metric for measuring products that pass quality assurance the first time was poor. Could this content, if delivered in a way that supported the user, affect that metric? She got information on that metric from the organization's data repository and started to work. To build the curriculum, she included not only the manager but also the organization's engineers, frontline leadership in the department, and people who created the product. She uncovered some disagreement on the way the content was applied, but she masterfully put together a learning experience that made all the stakeholders happy and could help affect the metric.

The final product was a combination of:

- Scenario-based e-learning experiences
- Leadership talking points for stand-up meetings (different prompts to ask about how product creation is going and what types of defects are being seen, and to help bridge the communication gap between product creators and leadership)
- A company-wide, "spot the defect" contest, based on the e-learning program with a link to the technical document explaining the defects

You may be thinking, that sounds great but it will never work in my organization. I know the feeling! I'm not going to sugarcoat it; this was a challenge to roll out for several reasons:

1. People didn't understand what we were trying to do. They couldn't wrap their heads around something that wasn't a PowerPoint deck.

2. This took more time to execute when the stakeholder really wanted the team to upload the deck and assign it to everyone in the area so they could be aware of the defects. I countered that I was sure everyone in the department was already aware of defects. So what? How would they be supported in trying to prevent them?

3. After talking about the various causes of the defects, the manager realized that the lighting in his area was different from the area where the part inspectors worked, which could also contribute to the defect issues.

We will talk about needs assessments later, but imagine if we hadn't had this conversation. Who knows what would have happened? For too many organizations, training is a scapegoat for management failures and crummy culture. Training can't fix environmental factors or a culture with a lack of accountability. Training also doesn't fix conversations leaders are scared to have with their direct reports.

The LXD Capabilities

You may be struggling still to see how learning experience design is defined or applied. It's a lot of information to digest. I had a random "shower thought" one day about mapping capabilities of learning experience design, so I put out a call on LinkedIn to see if others would be interested. I was overwhelmed by the response and ended up connecting with a fellow learning leader, Jeffrey Horne, who was on a similar crusade with his organization, Edward Jones. While Horne's team had different aspects of their roles than the team I led at my organization, the collaboration and conversation was valuable. I was surprised at the amount of overlap we had on the capabilities. To help operationalize learning experience design, Figure 1-1 breaks the LXD capabilities into three buckets (strategic, applied, and core) to shape and define the work we do. Let's go in depth to explore each level.

Figure 1-1. Learning Experience Design Capabilities

* Resource Management
* Lifelong Learning
* Trends and Innovation
* Proactive vs. Reactive

* Experience Design
* Accessibility and Inclusion
* Project Management
* Measurement
* Learning Technologies
* Knowledge Management

* Research
* Needs Assessment
* Relationship Management
* Learning Science
* Facilitation

Core LXD Capabilities

The core LXD capabilities are research, needs assessment, relationship management, learning science, and facilitation. To be a learning experience design practitioner, it is critical to have these capabilities because they provide a foundation for all the other capabilities. As folks continue to grow and master these core learning experience design capabilities, they will be able to check off the applied capabilities as well as the strategic capabilities.

Research

Often, people assume the word *research* means the academic sense. In the case of learning experience design, however, it means several other things. One is that you are willing to really dig deep for the learning experience. In the manufacturing example I shared, the learning experience designer knew that uploading a PowerPoint presentation into the LMS would at best waste people's time and at worst likely confuse them and do more harm than good. Research is critical to knowing the problem you are trying to solve and the population you are training and to creating a learning experience that supports both. Additionally, it's beyond just the training course, whether it is an in-person session, a virtual instructor-led training course, or an e-learning module. In the research phase, dive deeper and consider how you can set people up for success from exploring a drip campaign of content using spaced retrieval to creating a list of talking points for leaders to use when speaking to employees about the content; far too often, with the pressures of departments, many folks skip this step. Over the years, I've learned the hard way that while subject matter experts (SMEs) have good intentions, oftentimes they don't have key pieces of information. I like doing a task analysis, which I'll discuss more in the chapters to come.

Needs Assessment

This is easily one of the most important parts of learning experience design, but it sadly gets overlooked frequently, especially by folks new to the work that we do. By a needs assessment, I mean the act of digging in to see if a learning experience is really the right answer to the problem. I know throughout my career I've been treated as a short-order cook with stakeholders demanding a training program and wanting it tomorrow. In some environments, I've been able to push back and approach conversations from a place of curiosity to help the stakeholder with a solution, but I've been in plenty of roles where I had no such autonomy. Now that I lead a team, I encourage everyone on the team to be thoughtful and intentional during this step. Don't assume that a learning experience is needed, but use the opportunity to be a partner with the business. Often, stakeholders are told training is needed, and they are in a hurry to set it up and go back to their jobs.

While needs assessments aren't new to instructional designers, learning experience design principles should encourage you to go deeper when performing a task analysis. User experience (UX) designers use many techniques to create more robust data that help inform your design choices. This includes user interviews, which can go beyond a typical stopgap of using SMEs, to really empathizing and learning what problems users face and how we can solve them. Additionally, UX designers dig into a "day in the life" of users to consider factors that can also provide additional context of the problem. I'll explore this more of this in chapters 4 and 5.

Relationship Management

It is critical for learning experiences to be built in partnerships. I'll never forget one of the first emails I received when I was onboarding into a training manager role in a manufacturing setting. It was from the process engineering manager, who made an off-color comment about the current state of the training program. Instead of taking this comment negatively, I set up a meeting with him to talk. He quickly became one of my team's biggest champions as we tried to change the way learning and development was done at the organization. Thinking back to many of my missteps when creating training courses, they often failed due to lack of clarity of the content or lack of buy-in from stakeholders. It is a precarious situation when you're unsure how much to share. Also, depending on the organization, you may have the autonomy to manage your own project, or you may have a team project manager or an enterprise project management office. Dealing with people is fundamental to the success of any learning experience you build. If it weren't for people, we wouldn't have jobs. Imagine if robots took over the workforce; we'd have no one to train.

Learning Science

The incredible Clark Quinn (2021) argues that learning design is applied learning science, and I agree. If you are unable to design learning experiences to aid in the way that people learn, you are doing it wrong. In my opinion, this is a big reason why most higher education programs in learning and development are theory based; it is crucial for learning experience designers to understand the science behind learning. It's an interesting continuum because while you may have great content, it's possible to create the learning experience or produce it in a system that doesn't use learning science to its advantage. In chapter 8, I'll explore learning science as it pertains to learning technologies and how to implement them in your learning design process.

Facilitation

I heard Eddie Turner speak in 2018 about facilitation being the key to driving organizational change and business results, and it has stuck with me ever since. Thinking about learning experience design, isn't that exactly what we would like to do as well? *Facilitation* can be defined as the act of helping a group of people work together better, understand their common objectives, and plan how to achieve those objectives through various meetings or discussions. Whether it is working with subject matter experts or managing stakeholders' expectations, facilitation is key to learning experience design. It's a core capability because we often have a unique position in our organizations. We usually aren't on the front line, and we usually aren't in the C-suite. Because we are detached, we have the advantage of being able to ask questions we likely couldn't get away with otherwise. Facilitation skills allow us to be organizational detectives, and as you develop and mature in your facilitation style, you'll find that even the toughest exteriors can melt away when you can find common ground.

Reflection: Based on the outlined core capabilities, what do you think are your strengths and areas of opportunity?

Applied LXD Capabilities

The applied capabilities fall into seven buckets: experience design, accessibility and inclusion, project management, measurement, learning technologies, content design, and knowledge management. I wouldn't consider these capabilities for novices; although, you could easily specialize in any of these and have a robust career.

Experience Design

One of the most difficult tasks, especially for new designers, is to figure out the appropriate modality for the learning experience. Please note, I am not talking about learning styles here, but about how to determine what type of experience to create. While much of this book does refer to digital learning experiences, as someone who worked in manufacturing during the pandemic, I believe that it's misguided to assume that everything needs a digital product. The population I served in manufacturing had varying levels of technical proficiency. As the organization grew and we welcomed new folks, almost every week I met someone who couldn't use a computer. This is no exaggeration. I'll never forget one person who lifted their mouse up and pointed the laser to the screen, thinking that was the way to use it. My heart broke; had I not seen it with my own eyes, I would not have believed it.

I've made learning experiences that were signs hung above urinals, alerts in an enterprise software system, instructor-led training sessions, or small group discussions. My point is that it takes a competent learning experience designer to know what type of training will be most effective and how. Is there something that folks just need to be aware of? If it doesn't require a full learning experience, I recommend using a communication medium. Is there a task that could cost someone their employment if they can't perform it? That sounds like a case for a performance test. There is no magic bullet—each situation is as unique as the organization and the people we serve. The way to get better is through experience, and I always recommend building a network of other learning and development professionals to support you on your journey.

Accessibility and Inclusion

As learning experience designers, it is our responsibility to make sure the experiences we create not only can be used by everyone but are also open, inclusive, and accessible to all.

This is especially true in our digital learning experiences. For example, media such as videos should have captions and transcripts. Any images in digital learning experiences should have alternative text, also called alt text, which provides a text description of the image. It's also important to consider including captions and transcripts for synchronous learning experiences such as virtual instructor-led training courses or in-person training sessions. Furthermore, doing extensive usability testing for our learning technologies, auditing our language for inclusion, and setting up our products to be accessible from the start (so we don't have to retrofit) are things that should be considered. The best part of adding these elements is that they can be used by all, not just by people who may need additional support.

I will go into more depth about accessibility and inclusion in chapter 6, where I'll also discuss POUR, an acronym you should consider when creating learning experiences.

Project Management

Depending on the organization you work for, learning experiences may be managed by the learning designer or another group, such as a project manager in the learning and development function or by an enterprise specific project management office. For learning designers, managing projects can be tricky, especially if a lot of the work and follow-up needs to be done by others like subject matter experts or project sponsors.

The question that guides my project management philosophy is, "Who is doing what by when?" Often, this isn't as simple as it appears on the surface. The best learning experiences are always collaborative projects. Without the help of others through feedback and content, the learning experiences we create will not make an impact. Plus, stakeholder support can lead to better resources and buy-in across the organization. I will touch on a key component of project management, the scope agreement, in chapter 3.

Measurement

How do you know if your learning experience hit the mark? Often, learning experiences are created without specific metrics or key performance indicators in mind. Even worse, many experiences are created with no evaluation opportunity for the user to give us feedback; if there is an evaluation form, it may only ask questions that are superficial and provide no real indication of how users feel about the experience or if they can apply it to the work they do. While measurement often gets overlooked because it isn't as sexy as other elements of learning experience design, if you can't confidently say that you have provided users with practice opportunities in formative and summative assessments, what is the point of your learning experience? A content dump wastes users' time and costs the organization money. Additionally, how will you know if users were able to apply the content to their jobs? Feedback is important, and far too often the wrong questions are asked. I will go into more detail about measurement chapter 10.

Learning Technologies

How important are the technologies that we use to create learning experiences? I'd argue that too often, if learning designers have access to a particular e-learning authoring tool, they will try to build experiences in that tool all the time. A learning experience designer who has experience with the applied capabilities, on the other hand, can count on having multiple tools in their toolbox. In other words, they can focus on the content and the action that users will take before trying to figure out how to build the experience with learning technologies. Sometimes all that is needed is a performance support update on an organization's intranet instead of pushing out a full course to everyone in the organization.

I will go into more detail about learning technologies in chapters 5 and 8.

Knowledge Management

As organizations mature in their understanding of how to do jobs and document learning experiences that help provide support, knowledge management is critical to help create order so documents can be found and maintained. I'll never forget the horror I experienced when I discovered that a company I worked for was using the learning management system as a dumping ground for PowerPoint decks, technical documents, and other items with no order around the metadata and no structure among the files. They had done this for years, and by the time I came along, there were too many fires that I didn't know how to put out. The key component of knowledge management is that nothing lasts forever, so we must create a system for updating and maintaining information. Also, people need to know how to find the things they need to do their jobs, so considering taxonomies is important.

Reflection: Based on the outlined applied capabilities, what are your strengths and areas of opportunity?

Strategic LXD Capabilities

The last grouping is filled with the strategic capabilities of agility, resource management, lifelong learning, and proactivity and reactivity. To me, the highest level capabilities and often set you up for success in a leadership role, although you certainly don't need to be in leadership to use them. These capabilities are out of scope of this book; however, I'll briefly touch on them here and explore them again when I talk about what it means to be an LXD champion.

Agility

The rapid pace of change in this space is something that attracts me to the work, but it can also be difficult to keep up with. I call out trends and innovation specifically because I see many professionals fall victim to savvy claims and seduction by shiny new objects. It's one thing to explore a trend, but it's another to know when to adopt it for your setting. Strategic learning experience designers know that while something may seem like a magic fix for their organization's problems, there's also great value in doing due diligence before implementation.

Resource Management

Not every member of your team will have the same skill levels as a learning leader, so it can be difficult to balance projects against available resources. People are complex, and when you factor in workplace politics, it can be extremely challenging to allocate the right resources to the right project. Do you partner your best person with the challenging subject matter expert, or do you give a stretch assignment or growth opportunity to a person who is struggling? These decisions often have to be made quickly, and there may be big consequences for making the wrong choice.

Lifelong Learning

Many people say they value lifelong learning but then fail to follow through. Go to LinkedIn right now, search "lifelong learning," and look how many people have that in their headline. Talk is cheap, and I love to ask this question in job interviews: "How do you keep up with everything that goes on in learning and development?" I can tell very quickly when I've startled someone because they'll give a vague answer like LinkedIn or blogs, so I clarify and ask for more specifics.

Lifelong learning is so important to me that I tell team members to get out there to learn and I block calendar time weekly for them to do so. Seeing what others are talking about or working on can influence your learning experiences, if not immediately then in the future. I've worked in learning and development for my entire professional career, and I still don't know everything. That's what I think I love most about this field; I believe that an expert can admit they still are learning and growing. Lifelong learning helps identify trends, which can also help inform innovations.

Proactivity vs. Reactivity

In most organizations I've worked for, projects have come to us. I haven't had to "hit the pavement" to look for work. If we have functioning systems and are in positions where we have good partners, we should be able to be proactive in the work we do. When I led a team, in a previous role, I had strong relational equity with our information technology department. Having this was great because it not only helped with technology resources but gave me enough planning time to know about a large system change that was coming in six months. This afforded me the precious time I needed to get a plan in place and decide how to execute it. The system change was announced to the business about a month before it happened, and when my boss came to me with their pants on fire about the change, I could report that we already had a plan in motion.

Reflection: Based on the outlined strategic capabilities, what are your strengths and areas of opportunity?

Conclusion

Learning experience design is a way of creating learning experiences that focus on the content and the context of the system. LXD blends elements of human performance, educational psychology, industrial and organizational psychology, learning technologies, and user experience design to make a learning experience that focuses on what a user needs to do with new information to be successful in their job. It's more than pushing content; it's about the intentionality of everything we do to craft a learning experience. In the next chapter, I'll walk through my learning experience design process.

30/60/90 Plan

As you look to incorporate pieces of this process in your own work, consider the following 30/60/90 plan. The best plans are made by you and are specific to your own situation. This generic template is intended to get you thinking about how to apply this plan to your work.

30 days: Explore your own definition of LXD and the LXD capabilities.

60 days: Identify one or two LXD capabilities you'd like to work on and gather resources.

90 days: Iterate and reflect on what worked and what hasn't.

Chapter 2
The LXD Process

In this chapter, we will explore:
- The steps of my learning experience design process
- A brief description of each step

The learning experience design process will likely look different for you depending on your setting and experiences. My process is heavily influenced by my experiences in corporations, nonprofits, higher education, and consulting. It also blends many elements including human performance, instructional system design, user interface (UI) and user experience (UX) design, and marketing to create a repeatable and consistent experience. Whether you adopt the LXD process or not, I'm confident there are elements of this process you will want to implement in your own work or perhaps will encourage you to have conversations about the work you and your teams currently do.

The crux of the LXD process embraces the content along with the context. It also touches on the emotional engagement pieces in multiple places. Here are the fundamental steps to my LXD process:

1. The Request
2. The Kickoff
3. The Scope Agreement
4. The Shoes
5. The Funnel
6. The Product
7. The Red Pen
8. The Message

9. The Takeoff

10. The Results

This chapter will introduce these steps, and the chapters that follow will go further in depth into each one.

To help you visualize my LXD process and anchor it to something you are likely familiar with, in Figure 2-1, I have compared my process to ADDIE, a popular project management framework that is short for analysis, design, development, implementation, and evaluation.

Figure 2-1. The LXD Process Compared to ADDIE

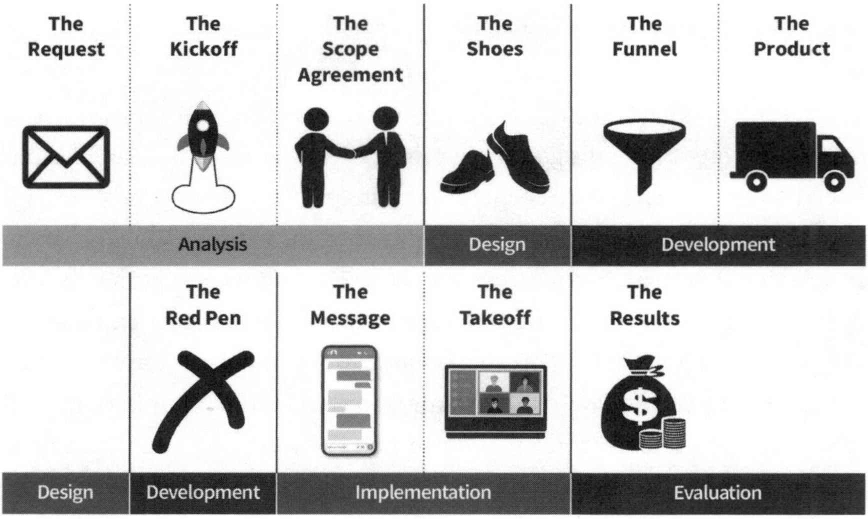

While ADDIE provides a nice starting framework to consider projects generally, it lacks the depth needed to guide talent development professionals in building learning experiences. (Note that while I'm not in the camp that thinks ADDIE is an instructional design model, I do believe it can be easily used to guide the development of everything from a new Lego set to a paper airplane.) In fact, if you were to ask a sample of talent development professionals to map their ADDIE processes for you, each would likely look very different from the others and from ADDIE. It is unlikely that many instructional designers use the same questions or processes for conducting a needs assessment, for example. The ADDIE process doesn't give prescriptive details for each step but serves more as general guidance.

Now, let's take a broad look at each step in the LXD process so you'll have some context for the more detailed dive into each step that will come later.

Reflection: While my LXD process improves upon ADDIE and reflects the unique needs of learning designers, it still won't account for every step and factor you'll encounter in your unique workplace. As you read this chapter, consider what your own process looks like. Then go back and compare my process to your own.

The Request

Regardless of your workplace, you will get many requests for projects. While I was in higher education, there were certain periods (usually right before an academic semester began) when I felt like I was the most popular person on campus. In corporate, it has been my experience that projects pop up if someone tells someone else that training is needed. In many workplaces, I'm finding that these requests can come from a variety of mediums: an old school "knock on the door" if people are working in the office, an email, a mysterious calendar invite for a virtual conference call, or even an instant message. Some folks expect talent development teams to be able to read their minds. Perhaps that's in jest, but I can remember one project when a stakeholder was angry with me because I didn't proactively start working on a training program for a new product that I knew nothing about.

The purpose of the request step is to set yourself and your stakeholder up for success. Regardless of how you get the request, use this step to seek to understand the message. Get more information before agreeing to meet with the stakeholder to discuss further. The information you gather will give you the data you need to understand the problem and provide an opportunity to investigate the issue before you decide to meet. For more information on this step, check out chapter 3.

The Kickoff

If you've done the work of gathering information during the request stage, you'll be prepared to have a kickoff meeting where you meet with the stakeholder to align on the project's success criteria. The kickoff is critical: This is how we set the expectations for the partnership. The best learning experiences are partnerships.

Use the kickoff meeting to be curious to the needs of the stakeholder while balancing what people need with what the organization needs. If we don't do it, no one else will. This step will also be explained in further detail in chapter 3. The information you collect directly from stakeholders will be combined with your own observations from the first step to result in the scope agreement, the next step.

The Scope Agreement

The scope agreement is the core of your project management and accountability for the creation of the learning experience, and it is the culmination of the first two steps. This is why all three are discussed in chapter 3. It's critical to get on the same page with your stakeholders, and I've found clearly outlining tasks and deliverables can be helpful. A scope agreement is a necessary component of my learning experience design process because it clearly allows you and your stakeholders to align on the tasks and responsibilities for creating the learning experience.

The Shoes

This step is about exploring someone's work by taking a walk in their shoes. Not only does this help build trust with users by involving them in the development of the learning experience, but it also builds relational equity because the employees taking the training course will help champion the learning experience when it is launched. Additionally, I've found that people are often in awe of the scope and complexity of the work that they do; until they have to explain it to me, they take it for granted. I once conducted a job analysis for a group of painters. It was clear in the beginning they didn't want to be there talking to me because they thought someone like me couldn't possibly understand the work they do. When the job analysis was complete, however, the painters had finally articulated the true scope of the decisions they made to do their jobs effectively and were able to share this insight with their leadership to advocate for more resources.

It is our job to empower the people who apply our training to their performance. Conducting a job or task analysis allows us to uncover obstacles people face in their jobs and highlight ways that we can help. A thorough job or task analysis can yield a lot of content, so how do you know what to include in the learning experience? This is explored in chapter 4.

The Funnel

By this point, you have the content, but what do you do with all of it? I funnel the content by keeping what is necessary and determining how it can be applied on the job. I use the task analysis and the key performance indicators (KPIs) set in the scope agreement to guide me. This isn't to say that I throw anything away. On the contrary, I like to keep everything. I've found that throwing away all the content a SME has given you is an easy way to upset them. I thank them for the content, and I keep it all in a folder in case more follow-up is needed further down the road. However, not all of the content has to go into the training course right now. Be ruthless; if something doesn't contribute to the goals, leave it out.

The funnel is important for setting your product up for success, so being able to take all the content you've received and funnel it through the goals of meeting your KPIs and enabling performance will help make the learning experience more succinct and targeted in what it is intended to do. This is covered in depth in chapter 4, alongside the shoes step, because your walk in a user's shoes will help you narrow down what's most useful to them.

The Product

My steps so far have covered the analysis and design phases of ADDIE. Now, we transition into the development phase. Not everything should be an e-learning program, so selecting the appropriate product solution is key. A great way to get guidance on what to create is by talking to people who execute the relevant task to understand what they use and what can be made for them. I'm a huge fan of performance support, as I find many products are made in a "one and done" fashion; that is, we expect 100 percent mastery after the learning experience, which is unfair to everyone.

It's critical to be a good partner to your stakeholders during product selection. Know that if you create an instructor-led training course, you may be held responsible for the administrative burdens of scheduling, confirming, and other associated tasks. When I worked in manufacturing, many employees worked 12-hour shifts, and I didn't want to schedule them for training sessions because the ebb and flow of the factory changed daily. A certain date in the future may sound good, but that would usually be the day when Murphy's Law would wreak havoc on the workflow forecasting. Having strong communication and partnerships throughout the whole process can help alleviate that burden on you.

With all the information you've gathered along with the way, which you have cut down to focus on the problem you are trying to solve, building the product should already be halfway done for you. Selecting the correct modality is important, and don't forget to leverage the users and seek to understand what works best for them whenever possible. This step is also going to vary the most from project to project, and that's why there are whole libraries of books about designing for different modalities to help you. Instead of getting into the weeds, this book will keep the focus on process; we'll focus specifically on three universal aspects of choosing a modality: UX/UI (chapter 5), accessibility and inclusion (chapter 6), and assessments (chapter 7).

The Red Pen

Now that you have created the perfect learning experience, you are done, right? Not so fast; it's key that you share your learning experience for feedback. I'm a fan of having the L&D team review the learning experience prior to sending it out to stakeholders. I also am a fan of receiving different types of feedback. Here are the pieces I look for during this stage:

- Team peer feedback on the experience
- Stakeholder feedback on accuracy
- Delivery review feedback

While you may think the learning experience you created is perfect, it is worthwhile to get feedback from other L&D peers and your SMEs. For this to be as streamlined as possible, you need to set expectations on what type of feedback you are looking for. If you don't, you may receive a fire hose of feedback and hurt feelings if you don't add requested music to the opening of a video. Make it known that your priority is accuracy. As for quality control, because it can be easy to get overwhelmed with too many details, I recommend having clear criteria and standards and trying not to deviate from them too much. Remember, it takes time for people to provide feedback, and you can't give someone a refund on their time. I will go into detail with examples in chapter 8.

Now that you've polished the product, it's time to discuss how people will know about what you've created.

The Message

Adults want to know the *why* behind something. Too often, learning experiences fail because people don't understand why they need to do something. I've seen so many mistakes and frustrations result from a lack of communication. If possible, I encourage you to consider pairing your learning experience with a communication campaign.

The message is also an opportunity to flex your creative muscles, so consider building a teaser trailer or launching a campaign around the product. Don't leave out the message (or the why) behind the creation of the learning experience because you assume people already know about it. Use this opportunity to explain why the learning experience was needed and how it will help people in their jobs. Once the message is crafted and sent out, you are ready for the takeoff. I will explore the message more in chapter 9.

The Takeoff

Are you someone who gets anxious right before a plane takes off from the tarmac? I certainly am. I usually close my eyes, say a little prayer, and nervously chew on my gum. Too often, once a product is launched, we turn to the next request and rinse and repeat. But once you roll out a learning experience, it's a great idea to observe the takeoff to make sure it's flying the way you'd hoped. If it's a live session, attend the first one to see how people respond. Ask for feedback after it rolls out. Maybe ask for an opportunity to walk the floor. If you don't have that opportunity, reach out to some users and set up a focus group.

Launching a learning experience shouldn't signal the end of the project. Use this phase to also consider if there are things you can do to support leadership in helping people apply the learning experience to their jobs. Consider creating assets for leaders, such as talking points for meetings or performance checklists. Also give leaders a way to give you any feedback they receive directly from users. I dive more into the takeoff in chapter 9.

The Results

While there are so many ways to evaluate learning experiences, I can't begin to tell you the impact Will Thalheimer's *Performance Focused Learner Surveys* (2022) had on me as a practitioner. Too often, I inherited weak organizational blanket evaluations, and if I wanted any real data, I would need to do my own follow-up with folks. Or worse, my organization would rely on a net promoter score, which was the departmental feel-good metric. In this process, with all the work you've done up to this point, hold yourself to a higher standard than a vanity metric. Net promoter scores tell you nothing about whether someone was able to apply the content to their job, their motivation to do so, or if they have any questions applying the content.

In his book, Thalheimer (2022) mentions some amazing questions, especially through the lens of motivation and performance. Thalheimer argues that instead of relying on an ambiguous number-based Likert scale (or rating between 1 and 5) to anchor the scale with a description of what each number means (for example, 1 = "I didn't learn anything useful" or "I required additional information or support to complete the task"). I took this advice when using Microsoft Forms to build evaluations at a past organization. Because Microsoft Forms automatically collected the name of the person who was filling out the form, if someone indicated they needed additional support, we could pull that information and help them or forward it to their leadership. This practice helped our department build relational equity and support across the company just by asking a question and following up. It was pivotal for my role specifically, as I was building a department up from nothing by myself, and it was important to me to provide value back to the organization. I will dive deeper into evaluation in chapter 10.

Conclusion

There you have it—my learning experience design process from request to results. Going back to your notes and your own process, how did we align? How did we differ? Are there aspects you want to try?

30/60/90 Plan for the LXD Process

As you look to incorporate pieces of this process in your own work, consider the 30/60/90 plan for this chapter. The best 30/60/90 plans are made by you and are specific to your own situation. This one is a general template to get you thinking about how you can apply this to your work.

30 days: Start planning for aspects you want to apply.

60 days: Try different elements in your next learning experience creation.

90 days: Iterate and reflect on the changes and keep experimenting.

Chapter 3

The Request, the Kickoff, and the Scope Agreement

In this chapter, we will explore:

- ◉ Techniques to take a request and gather data to determine if training is needed
- ◉ Strategies for organizing a kickoff meeting to gain input from stakeholders
- ◉ A guide to create a scope agreement

I've always loved the analysis part of any project because it gives me the opportunity to really understand the nuances of the organization. In my LXD process, I consider the request, the kickoff, and the scope agreement to be fundamental parts of an analysis, and if you can build a solid foundation with them, much of the work on the project will be done for you. In this chapter, we will go through the request, the kickoff, and the scope agreement in more detail.

Reflection: While each part of the process is important, this one really helps frame how the rest of the experience goes. On the surface at this stage, we just know there is a "problem" and are seeking to understand what the problem is. Before diving in, take a moment to reflect on your own intake process.

The Request

One aspect of our role as talent development professionals is to battle everyone's assumptions about education. Because our organizations are filled with folks who have some form of formal education (from K–12 to doctorates), people often think what we do is easy. They think that we just need to wiggle our noses to put something together. However, it is our job to ask questions to help determine what is really needed. Let's explore two examples of the types of people who send us training requests: the prescriber and the "spray and pray."

The Prescriber

This person needed the learning experience yesterday. They are often transactional, think of speaking to you as a "to-do," and have no time for formalities. They need you to make a training program, and that's the end of the discussion. You should instantly know what to do. Throughout my career, I've dealt with many prescribers, and one of the pitfalls I see (especially from folks new to learning experience design) is to put on a customer service hat and serve the prescriber their desired order. A question I want you to ponder when you receive a request from the prescriber is this: If you serve them their order, who are you really helping in the organization? Will you help the intended audience? Will you help only the prescriber? Maybe you won't help anyone.

The Spray and Pray

The attitude of this person is "I did the work for you already." This person at least realizes that most talent development departments have massive workloads, so they want to help. Maybe they made a PowerPoint presentation and expect you to get it over the finish line by uploading it to the LMS and making sure everyone sees it. This is what I call "spray and pray," or the notion that a learning experience is an evergreen, one-size-fits-all product, and that participation is simply a requirement of working at an organization. With learning experiences like this, it's no wonder that people often avoid learning experiences until the last possible minute. That's right, they would rather work than go through your learning experience. There is an amazing quote by Michael Allen (2020), the creator of the successive approximation model (SAM), that I love so much I share it on my email signature at work. Allen said, "If content were enough, we'd only have libraries and not schools." To me, that speaks volumes about the importance of what we do in learning experience design because we help connect the dots. We are the ones who translate content into activities, campaigns, job aids, or whatever else we can to make sure that the content can be applied and used to help enable learning in our organizations.

More often than not, people who send a "spray and pray" request have their hearts in the right place. They are likely getting pressure from their higher-ups or another stakeholder to pass along the hot potato.

Becoming a Process Expert

Whether you are dealing with the prescriber, the "spray and pray," or any other stakeholder, remember that you are the learning experience design process expert. You can turn this request around, and you owe it to the people you serve in your organization to do so. No matter what the request is or who it comes from, I handle it in the same way; I take control of the ship.

First, I start with a simple thank you. I realize this isn't revolutionary advice, but you would be shocked by how much a simple thank you matters. I'll go into relational equity more later in this chapter, but just know that even if the project sounds dreadful or like something a learning experience can't solve, you have to establish a strong working relationship to get buy-in on your ideas. I specifically like to thank the requester for their interest and for bringing the issue to my attention.

Next, I explain directly that the team has a way of managing our projects and we need additional information before scheduling it from a project management perspective. I've experienced many times that if I'm too nice, I will lose the battle every time. Be direct. If I get push-back here, I like to point out other areas of the business that use project management queues and planning, such as human resources or finance, and because our work is a shared service for the entire business, we must plan our resources strategically so we can partner and assist as many folks as possible. The keyword you are looking for here is partnerships.

Finally, and this is good practice regardless of the setting, I come from a place of curiosity to guide the requester to our intake form to set up a kickoff meeting. I want them to know I care and I genuinely want to learn more. In this phase of the process, you won't have enough information to create an impactful learning experience. Typically, you have just one person's perspective—the person sending you the information. Throughout the learning experience design process, I want to talk to other people who will be affected by the learning experience. I find that if I get pushback, I will advocate for the users, saying it may be helpful to see it from their perspectives. Doing that can convince someone to push the project through.

At this point, I direct the requester to our project intake form. Now I will warn you that your questions can make or break this project. If there are too many questions, stakeholders may not fill out the form. If there are not enough questions, you may not be able to determine if this is a situation that can be solved by a learning solution. In that case, your kickoff meeting will simply waste the time of you and the L&D team. Also, I've learned if someone really pushes back hard on a project intake form, their reaction can give you some much-needed insight into what it will be like working with them on this project. The incredible Cathy Moore, the author of *Map It* (2017) and the creator of a process called action mapping, has some wonderful questions for you to consider for your intake form and kickoff meeting. I've taken inspiration from her work and blended some business needs into the intake form that I use. Here are some of the questions I recommend and why they are important:

1. **How should I contact you?** While getting contact information is self-explanatory (Who is requesting this, and how do they prefer to be contacted going forward?), don't assume you know the answers. Some people want to be emailed, some instant messaged, and other people still prefer a phone call.

2. **What is the purpose of the learning experience you want created?** You can get a good sense of what someone is thinking with this question. Be wary when you see the phrases "people need to know x" or "people aren't doing y." Often, you will get superficial answers, but that is OK because you can dive into it further in the kickoff meeting.

3. **What business problem do you intend to solve with this learning experience?** This is one of my favorite questions because it asks the requester to pause and relate their request back to the greater organization. Sometimes people stumble with this one, and I've even seen "not applicable" as a response. It's a good practice to know what your organization's business priorities are. For example, are there annual organizational goals? Is the institution leaning into diversity, equity, and inclusion (DEI) initiatives? This is a great question to ask specifically from a resource planning perspective. If the answer ties into a direct business problem that has been on the agenda for the quarter or the year, you have an opportunity to prioritize the project over others that maybe aren't being given attention and resources. Furthermore, going back to the emotional hook that learning experience design helps create, wrapping the learning experience around the business problem can make the value of the learning experience (what is in it for them) clear to the people who will participate, and it can help provide an emotional connection for why it matters.

4. **Who are the stakeholders who need to be involved in the creation of this learning experience?** If the only stakeholder is the requester, this is a red flag. In the kickoff meeting, you'll want to cast a wide net and include others, if possible. However, you also don't want to have too many people involved; it is a delicate balance. Three to five people can offer good cross-functional representation without getting too many cooks in the kitchen.

5. **Have you taken any other actions to improve job performance?** So many project requests I've received throughout my career have been made in reaction to someone making a mistake. Sometimes a learning experience may be leveraged in a punitive way. This is not a good reason for a learning experience—we don't want what we create to have a punitive lens; we want it to be supportive. You should get a good sense of what has been tried in the past to gain an historical perspective of the problem. Don't be surprised, however, if they say, "not applicable." This question often gives stakeholders pause, and if you decide to take a kickoff meeting without the information, it will often come up later in discussion.

Frequently, the questions covered in the request phase to gather more information don't always get asked. For many of us, it may seem like organizations blame training for every problem yet assume more training will fix all problems. The purpose of this step is to position yourself and your department as a professional service to the business. Other parts of the organization likely have a workload and intake or project management process, and you deserve one too. Having a process can help curb the people who act like the "sky is falling" and come in red hot, wanting training now.

The Kickoff

After you have had a chance to go through the information provided either via an intake form, like I use, or your own methods, it's important to then schedule a kickoff meeting. Be intentional with who you invite. If you received answers on the intake form that were straightforward, then perhaps you should invite the stakeholder and one or two people from the learning and development team. If you will be asking hard questions, you may need to invite someone senior to the stakeholder. This is as much of an art as it is a science, and it's a balance that is highly dependent on the relational equity you may or may not have built in the organization. Regardless, the kickoff is critical and will set the expectations for the partnerships. For the kickoff meeting, I lean into the teachings of Cathy Moore (2017), who recommends action mapping. Action mapping, according to Moore, "is a streamlined process to design training in the business world."

Specifically, the action mapping process helps you:

- "Commit to measurably improving the performance of the business."
- "Identify the best solution to the performance problem."
- "Identify if a learning experience is truly necessary and create realistic practice opportunities." (Moore 2017)

I love action mapping because it works. I have worked in places such as call centers and manufacturing facilities, and do you know what they love? Data and metrics. Both environments live or die by their data and metrics, so if you can map learning experiences to data and metrics, it elevates your value to the business.

Because you may not have received good data from the intake form, a great lead-in to the kickoff starts by asking the question, "How will this affect the bottom line?" Time has a price in our organizations. Imagine the cost of a one-hour mandatory compliance training program to an organization of 1,000 people. If the average wage per hour is $25, the cost of the training program in time alone for the end users is at least $25,000, which does not account for the time of the talent development team, the cost of learning technologies, and so on. This type of example can help get the wheels turning for the stakeholders. You may see two different reactions here: sheer terror or eagerness. The people who experience terror will start second-guessing themselves and may reconsider if they are pushing the project too hard; the eager stakeholders think that the money is a good investment back to the business.

Therefore, setting an initial metric is a great activity. Help the stakeholder brainstorm what metric they think will be influenced by creating a learning experience. This may be something new for them, and you may need to be patient during this process. From my experience in manufacturing, there were several potential metrics, including yield of product, damage percentage of product, and on-time delivery of product to the customer. After the metric is agreed upon, pivot to build the key performance indicator (KPI). According to Moore's action mapping, this KPI becomes a North Star for the learning experience. If the content doesn't help this metric, that piece of content isn't needed.

What If Training Isn't Needed?

As the talent development expert at your organization, you should speak up if training isn't needed. Not every problem should be solved with training. In fact, training is not a substitute for an organization with a lack of accountability. Multiple asks for training can sometimes be made in lieu of having a conversation with an individual or department or, most often, when communication is needed instead.

The kickoff is a vital opportunity to be a business partner. I like going to these meetings assuming nothing and asking questions. Come from a place of curiosity. Here are some of the questions I like to ask during a kickoff, but be ready for some confused looks. Answers may not be readily available.

- What tells you there is a problem? What data led you to that conclusion?
- Have you had a chance to talk to the people who execute this task for us, or is this something you've heard about second hand?
- What does success look like when executing this task?
- What type of support do folks currently have with this task?

A kickoff meeting is an opportunity to set up a discovery call with your stakeholder, which allows them to describe their problem and goals and allows you time to ask necessary questions. Use this time as an opportunity to be a business consultant; ask questions that the stakeholder may not have considered, such as how success will be measured, how people currently execute this task, and why they aren't currently doing it as desired. A kickoff meeting should help pave the way to determining if a learning experience needs to be created or if someone simply needs to have a tough conversation.

I was approached by a possible client for a consulting project to create a nutrition training program for their staff in an assisted living facility. I asked the client how they knew this was a problem. They shared that a staff member had given a banana to a resident when that resident had a potassium restriction in their diet. While the resident ended up being OK, the administration was alarmed by the mistake and decided nutrition training was needed. They asked my potential client to seek out a freelancer. I asked for more information about the incident, specifically if we knew why the staff member gave the resident a banana. The client looked at me, stunned. They couldn't answer the question and admitted sheepishly that they were following orders to seek out a person to create a training course. By having this conversation, I encouraged the client to dig deeper to determine if it was a one-off mistake (which could be remedied by having a conversation with the staff member), an environmental issue (such as a lack of readily available snacks for residents based on dietary needs), or burnout (Was this person filling in for someone else or working a double shift and not making a good decision?). Training can't replace having a conversation about performance with a staff member. It can't fix an environment or resource issue like the availability of appropriate snacks for residents with special dietary needs. Training can't fix burnout in a situation where people may have to quickly fill in for someone or where staff are overworked.

The kickoff is a meeting with the project's stakeholders to understand more about the complexities of the problem. There are many times in this process when you may decide not to go any further if you determine training won't solve a problem or if a problem isn't ready for a training component. That's OK; in fact, that's actually a win because you have saved the organization time and money by not rolling out a solution that won't solve the problem. If you do conclude that you can help, proceed to the scope agreement.

The Scope Agreement

The scope agreement is useful for outlining a charter and clearly defining what you and the stakeholders will do. You can't and shouldn't have to do everything in the learning experience design process. There should be some give and take and clear criteria and tasks along the way. Table 3-1 presents a list of dos and don'ts I recommend when creating a scope agreement.

Table 3-1. Dos and Don'ts When Creating a Scope Agreement

Do: Consider signing a memorandum of understanding (MOU). This is a document that clearly defines what each party is responsible for (such as SMEs for content feedback and LXD for content develop-ment). This is an important piece of your scope agreement.	**Don't** create a scope agreement where someone doesn't have "skin in the game." It's critical that everyone has a clear role. If someone doesn't have a role, there is no reason why they should help the success of the project.
Do: Set up a communication method before the project begins so people know how communication will be shared. Say, for example, "We will have a Microsoft Teams channel for the project, and I'll tag you throughout the development pro-cess if additional information is needed."	**Don't** let a few small speed bumps rattle your confidence in the project. **Don't** be afraid to escalate issues as they come up.
Do: Consider how the project can stay on track and have a plan in place in case things get off track. Know which parts of the project you can adjust if you need to.	**Don't** back down if the MOU terms are violated. I have a phrase for projects like this: "Stuck in the sludge." Say you've received no feedback from SMEs after many attempts to contact them. The project must not be that important to them, so move it to "sludge" (as in, depri-oritize it) and go to your next project.
Do: Keep a log throughout the project for you to reflect on later as lessons learned. They are often transferable to other projects.	

When creating scope agreements, consider the norms of the organization. Keep it simple and targeted, and avoid superfluous language. No matter how you design it, a core element of the scope agreement is a work plan. For simplicity, I usually format the work plan as a table, calling out who (stakeholders or the L&D team) is responsible for what during which phase (Figure 3-1). This, paired with an MOU, sets you up for success when managing the project overall.

Figure 3-1. Example of a Work Plan From a Scope Agreement

Work Element	Steps and Responsibilities	Approximate Timeline
Project kickoff	Vendor and sponsor • Meet to review objectives, scope of work, and planned deliverables	1 hour
Storyboarding	Sponsor • Provide additional information about content • Provide feedback on storyboards and revisions • Sign off on storyboards to transition into e-learning development Vendor • Analyze provided information to create storyboards for modules • Make revisions based on feedback • Finalize storyboards	1 week
Development	Sponsor • Provide feedback • Meet with vendor to discuss recommendations Vendor • Develop module in the LMS • Make revisions as needed	1 week
Project completion	Sponsor • Meet to discuss project experience and satisfaction with deliverables Vendor • Provide final deliverables pending sponsor approval	1 week to provide final modules with project management and style guide Plus 1 hour for project debrief

When considering scope agreements, you may also want to think about the way you manage projects in general. Some organizations have an enterprise project management office or a project manager to help with this step. I've mostly managed projects myself throughout my career, with a lot of flops. While there are several tools available to help you manage projects and scope, I recommend using what you have available to you. I've used tools from Jira to Trello (Figure 3-2); as long as it works and the content is updated, that's what matters.

Figure 3-2. Example of a Kanban-Inspired Project Management Board in Trello

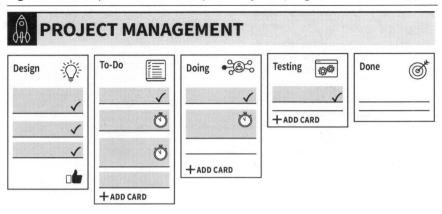

The scope agreement serves to align on the work that needs to be done and to ensure the learning experience design process is a partnership. The importance of relational equity and being a good partner can't be understated. The best learning experiences are partnerships, and the scope agreement lays out how to accomplish that goal. Finally, because scope agreements are great ways to document who is doing what and by when, they can also identify the consequences if a component is missed. I am ruthless about moving projects over to the "sludge" standing if I don't get the engagement I need from my partners. Remember, the best learning experiences are partnerships, and the scope agreement helps build a foundation of transparency and trust so that we can focus on providing the users of the learning experience with the best possible product.

Conclusion

Remember, the request, kickoff, and scope agreement are essential to setting your project up for success. Depending on your organization, you may not have a formal process, but if they are not done, you risk setting yourself up to battle scope creep and do a disservice to yourself from an assessment and evaluation standpoint because you won't be able to assess and evaluate what you can't measure. These critical phases can also help with accountability if a project goes sideways during development.

30/60/90 Plan

As you look to incorporate pieces of this process in your own work, consider this 30/60/90 plan. The best 30/60/90 plans are made by you and are specific to your own situation. This one is general to get you thinking about how you can apply this to your work.

30 days: Explore your own needs assessment process.

60 days: Identify something to try or improve.

90 days: Iterate and reflect on what has worked and what hasn't.

Chapter 4
The Shoes and the Funnel

In this chapter, we will explore:

- Why you should use a task analysis
- How funneling provides you with the content you need to include in a learning experience

How critical is a task analysis (the shoes step) to the success of a learning experience? I argue that this step is a core component of your design, alignment, and assessment. While task analysis is something I like to do when I'm creating a learning experience, the concept of task analysis isn't new. If you dig into literature, research, and articles about task analysis, you'll see how it is discussed in instructional design. Much of the literature suggests task analysis can make an impact on content creation when compared with content that lacks a task analysis (Tofel-Grehl and Feldon 2013). I think it's so important, but there aren't enough people doing it. Too often, people skip the task analysis and just use the content that subject matter experts (SMEs) provide. In my experience, that can be a slippery slope, and even if well intentioned, it can lead us to miss the mark.

One of my first solo instructional design projects when I worked at Amazon was to develop customer service associate training for the Amazon Santa application, which allowed kids to build a wish list on Amazon's website that would be sent to Santa on their behalf. I'll never forget meeting the program manager for the product. When I looked him up in staff directory,

I was immediately intimidated by his level in the company. He told me this program would be the digital product of the year and how many users they anticipated. He made it sound like it was the most important project of that quarter. I started to feel the pressure, so I took all the content he gave me and built an e-learning course that discussed troubleshooting and basic usability of the application. Sadly, I took this information for granted. I didn't take the time to walk in the shoes of the people taking the training course or using the application.

To make a long story short, I created a mandatory 15-minute e-learning course during the busiest quarter of the year to make the stakeholder happy. I did not dig into how many contacts the business received about the wish list, and I did not talk to customer service agents. All I cared about was making the stakeholder happy. Needless to say, it was an epic fail and an extremely low percentage of customer contacts for the quarter.

The failure was in the sense that the training I created was focused on everything a customer service associate should know about the product, according to a passionate SME. I didn't do any work to understand what the associates already knew about the product, explore how they could get information about the product in the system they worked in, or go beyond the SME to understand the general number of customer contacts around similar types of contacts. Looking at it from a money and time perspective, I made a mandatory training during a busy time of the year for the business when time not focused on helping customers was in short supply. Also, if I'm being brutally honest, even the design of what I made was a fail because it was built directly into the LMS with words, more words, and of course bullet points.

When this information was shared with me, I knew immediately that I was likely on my way out the door and I should look for a new job. My supervisor, however, used it as a teaching moment: You represent the user but not always the stakeholder. Do what works for the user. This was a formative experience for me, and even describing it now gives me some nausea as I re-experience those nervous feelings from that project.

The Task Analysis (Shoes)

So, what are some of the benefits of task analysis? According to Clark and colleagues (2007), it includes identifying knowledge representations, analyzing and verifying data acquired, and formatting results for intended application. Let's deconstruct each one:

- **Identify knowledge representations.** It's been my experience that even if they're minimal, there are usually discrepancies between what a SME says someone should know versus what people who do the job everyday actually need to know. There are a many reasons why this happens. For instance, SMEs bring a wealth of experience and expertise that can make it difficult for them to break down what someone does daily. Also, SMEs may be in organizational positions that aren't in production, such as in a management or supervisory capacity. A task analysis allows you to gather information known about the task and determine how it is performed on the job by someone doing the work. This analysis goes beyond a SME's expertise and asks how the task can actually be performed. Always keep in mind the metaphor of walking in their shoes—that's why it's the shoes step.

- **Analyze and verify data acquired.** Have you ever considered if the information provided is accurate? I have so many examples I could share from when I've taken the SME at their word and not verified accuracy. It may not always be ill intentioned; perhaps the SME doesn't have the most up-to-date information via policies and procedures, or things changed since the last time they conducted the task. Completing a full task analysis and authenticating the data beyond just the person providing the information allows for more alignment and verification of the data. It also allows you to solicit more ideas around cues and errors that occur in each step.

- **Format results for intended application.** What does success look like? By leveraging a task analysis, the performance criteria writes itself. My main case for taking the time to create a task analysis for any learning experience is simple: A thorough task analysis will determine the performance criteria for a task. I'll even go a step further to say that it practically writes your learning objectives for you (and with a stronger performance lens).

When I worked in manufacturing from 2020 to 2022, our plant grew its headcount rapidly to ramp up production. With so many people joining the organization and working in niche roles within specific departments, it became clear during many of the learning experiences designed for operations employees that the instructional designers and the learners themselves may not have an overarching view of how complex an issue was. For example, if someone performed quality assurance, they might not understand the material constraint that a machinist may have in a particular value stream.When the team I led adopted action mapping and the process outlined in chapter 3, we often found that we were stumped on the context piece. We knew something needed to be done, but we wanted to be respectful of any time being taken away from production. We looked for a "Goldilocks" approach, and when we shifted our thinking to problem solving and the demonstration and application of skills, it helped us determine what needed to be added into the learning experience. In other words, we became business partners to help determine the need in the area so we could align the problem back to the needs of the business. In the case of this organization, by sitting in the operations portion of the business, I could lean into my other operations leaders to gain clarity around critical metrics for additional context. We also advocated for a variety of potential solutions and truly could do that by leveraging our operations partners and considering multiple factors of why the problem was occurring.

There is value in anchoring the user in the scenario (explaining who they are and their role). I can recall one specific project that flopped because the stakeholders would not budge on their desire for the content to go out to a broader audience. The learner evaluations from that project let us know loud and clear that the content didn't apply to them. In this case, there were many missteps including not appropriately aligning with stakeholders and leadership and not taking the time to focus on the problems that the content would solve. Using a scenario to walk through the task together may have illuminated some of these issues before the training program was even developed.

Task analysis can become your most valuable product (MVP) in the learning experience design process (Table 4-1). It is a multipurpose tool that allows you to align on the content, verify performance criteria, identify common mistakes, and build empathy for a user through the problems in each step of the task. In the next chapter, we will explore UX and UI principles for LXD.

Table 4-1. Example of a Task Analysis and Clarifying Questions

Steps	What are the actions one has to do to complete the task?
Performance Measures	How do they know they did the task correctly?
Tools, Equipment, and Materials	What do they need to use to execute the task?
Required Knowledge and Skills	What knowledge do they need to apply to complete the task?
Safety	Are there any safety concerns?
Decisions	What questions do they need answered, internally or externally, to complete the task?
Errors	How do people mess up during this step?

There are many ways to conduct a task analysis:

- Observe the person doing the task and take notes. Then talk to them about filling in any gaps that may exist.
- Compare current knowledge management documents such as standard operating procedures (SOPs). Try to fill in Table 4-1, and compare it to the work someone does. This is an excellent way to find gaps.
- Fill in Table 4-1 with the person doing the task, virtually walking through each section together.

Regardless of how a task analysis is conducted, it is important to get more than one opinion on it. If possible, base the task analysis on a few people, and then send it to a broader audience for review. This helps eliminate biases and ensures more uniformity in the way the task is done.

Reflection: Even if you feel like you've never done a task analysis before, you likely have without knowing when you are collecting and synthesizing content. While in practice, task analysis can be more in the flow as you talk to people and take inventory of previous material. Reflect on your current process for this step and consider how to use task analysis in your work.

In my opinion, the content collected from a task analysis can greatly help your learning experience. In particular, the column where you list errors is a gold mine for assessments such as work-based scenarios. Knowing where folks fumble can also shed light on any gaps in the environment or knowledge management, which you can then share with stakeholders when appropriate. If you need to see an example to make it stick, Table 4-2 provides an example task analysis for a few steps of conducting a pre-trip check for a semitruck.

When developing a task analysis, procedural steps should become clear and the analysis should provide an opportunity to break down each step. I encourage you to consider personas through the lens of situations and scenarios that are important characteristics to success in the KPI identified during the kickoff meeting instead of relying on traditionally distinguished audiences. The personas, or representations of users based on research, are task focused. This allows you to extrapolate what is needed in the learning experience and map it back to the agreed upon metrics from the kickoff.

The Funnel

At this point, you should have a great deal of content and you may be wondering how you determine what to use versus what not to use. This is where the idea of a funnel comes into your process—you want to look back at your KPI and success metrics and what you and your stakeholders agreed that you were helping to create for the organization. Put simply, if the content doesn't align to what the person will do because of the learning experience, funnel it out.

Table 4-2. Example of a Task Analysis Excerpt: Conducting a Pretrip Check for a Semitruck

Steps	Performance Measure	Tools and Equipment	KSAs	Safety	Decisions	Errors
• Inspect lighting devices and reflectors	• Headlights function (on, bright, dim) • Turn signals work (left and right) • Hazard lights function • Brake lights function (on truck and trailer, if applicable) • Check reflectors for reflection	• Flashlight for reflector • Pretrip checklist • Electronic log-in device (ELD) • Paper and pencil for notes	• Components of pre-trip checklist • Basic usage components of truck	• OSHA guidelines • Parking brake is on • Safety vest is worn • Steel-toe boots are worn	• Did I note in the ELD that I've started my pretrip? • Have I tested all the functions of the headlights? • Are any bulbs close to being burnt out that need to be repaired? • Have I documented any issues for my pretrip report?	• Skipping inspection of any lighting device or reflector • Not noting any potential dimming bulbs • Not noting any issues with the vehicle's lighting devices and reflectors

If you encounter pushback in this step, allow me to introduce you to the brilliant work of Gary Dickelman (1996; Figure 4-2). According to him, you should consider four criteria to create an environment that will increase performance (which is most likely the metric agreed to during the kickoff meeting and scope agreement):

Figure 4-2. Highway to the Performance Zone Adapted From Dickelman (1996)

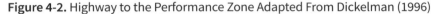

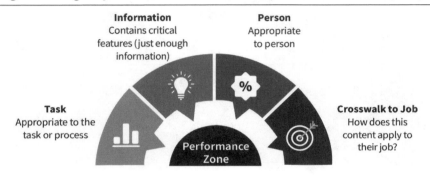

- **Task:** Ensure the content is appropriate to the task or process. Another great skill set we bring to the table while creating learning experiences is to push SMEs to define their jargon and alphabet soup (or what happens when you get a list of acronyms and shorthand you don't understand). Anyone going through the learning experience should understand what the acronyms mean.
- **Information:** Funnel the content to make sure it's needed to perform the task, and map it back to the metric set in the kickoff meeting and scope agreement. If content is extraneous and not needed to conduct the task, kick it to the curb. If stakeholders insist on including the removed content, there are other places you can put the information, such as in the communication section or metadata.
- **Person:** It should be clear through initial conversations who the intended audience is; however, you may need to add to the content or refine it based on information yielded from the task analysis. We want to enable the appropriate people to do their jobs more effectively.

- **Crosswalk to job:** Be diligent when "crosswalking" the content to the job. Bring in the information you have about business goals and objectives, KPIs and metrics, and so on. Paint the picture of why the content matters to the job.

The funnel is also the stage when I start to storyboard and gather ideas about what the learning modality and product will be. It's a great opportunity to touch base with your stakeholders to show them your ideas. I've often found they get excited when you show them a job or task analysis and funnel down what the task is and how it should be executed. You may discover a disagreement between what the person identified in the task analysis thinks and what leadership or stakeholders think. As tempting as it is to intervene, this is a disconnect between workers and management that you may have to punt back to them to work out among themselves. You just need to let them know that expectations are misaligned, which could also be contributing to the performance issues at hand.

Have you ever been in a job that had different expectations from leadership than what you experienced on the job? I'd say many of us can relate to that; think of your work in these situations as a stepping stone to fixing the problem by highlighting the misalignment to your stakeholders. Just keep in mind that in these situations, training is not the whole solution.

Funneling can also help you leverage learning science to create the best learning experience for the user. From using motivational techniques to get users excited to exploring spaced practice and reflection, learning science can help you shape the product you create. As Clark Quinn says in his book *Learning Science for Instructional Designers* (2021), we need to go beyond creating products that only enable users to recite facts; we need to empower them to make better decisions. We can do that by leveraging learning science.

Conclusion

It is necessary to put yourself in the shoes of others to understand what they are doing and to truly get a sense of their constraints and day-to-day work. Too often, if you rely only on SMEs, you'll get only a portion of the story.

Additionally, lean into all the work you've done up to this point to keep the content in the learning experience tight and targeted. The funneling stage will help you determine what stays and what can be filtered out.

30/60/90 Plan

As you look to incorporate pieces of this process in your own work, consider this 30/60/90 plan. The best 30/60/90 plans are made by you and are specific to your own situation. Here is a general template to get you thinking about how you can apply this to your work.

30 days: Consider how you put yourself in the shoes of your users and identify one new aspect you'd like to try.

60 days: Look retrospectively at a project that you would like new perspectives on or try the new aspect in a new project.

90 days: Iterate and reflect on what has worked and what hasn't.

Chapter 5
The Product: UX and UI

In this chapter, we will explore:

- User experience (UX) principles and how they relate to LXD
- User interface (UI) principles and how they relate to LXD

We've made it to the step in the process that people either love or hate: creating the learning experience product. Up to this point, I've focused on the substance of the learning experience—what the KPIs are and what tasks we are going to help people improve. My late Granny, who I miss dearly, was known for being a blunt woman; she gave me sage advice about dating that I think I can apply to the product step: "Just because it looks good doesn't mean it has substance."

I've seen an uptick in e-learning examples specifically being shared in portfolios that focus more on the aesthetics than the content. Many have copied and pasted content that has no value to the performance criteria (if you can even assume performance criteria from what's presented). In this chapter, however, I want to explore the usability and aesthetic facets of developing learning experiences because they also matter. This chapter won't necessarily dive deep into visual design but will focus more on exploring UX and UI for learning experience design.

But first, let's take a moment to define *UX* and *UI*. Both terms spring from the software development and design world. UX stands for user experience. Cognitive scientist Don Norman (2013), defines UX as encompassing all aspects of a user's interaction within a product. UX design is about the process of developing and improving the quality of the interaction or product. It's not about visuals, but it concerns the overall feel of the experience. Unlike UX, UI—user interface—is focused more on the aesthetic of the learning experience, how it looks and sounds as users interact with it.

Reflection: As you go through this chapter, consider your own approach to UX and UI and reflect on how you apply them in your work. You may already be doing it without realizing.

UX

Despite working in different departments, I believe that user experience (UX) professionals and learning experience designers share similar goals: to create products that solve problems and that people will use. For many UX designers, this can mean an e-commerce application, a marketing campaign, or a healthcare system. For learning experience designers, this can mean software training, task-based guidance of a process, or leadership development training. Here are some additional shared goals both UX and learning experience designers have:

- Create products from a holistic strategy, not focused only on aesthetics.
- Conduct user research to understand how people accomplish tasks and what they need to be successful.
- Test and evaluate products to make iterative design improvements.

If you read those bullet points and thought that maybe you don't do those things in your learning experiences, that is OK. I'd argue that not enough people do them, and there is a list of reasons why. There are times I haven't done them either. Let's explore more.

First, many learning and development departments are set up as course factories where training programs are mass produced. Like servers in a restaurant, L&D professionals find themselves taking the orders of the organization to serve up a "fast food" learning experience that may fill a need but not truly nourish the underlying issue. There are so many reasons why this happens—one being an ineffective learning leader.

Something that surprised me when I transitioned into learning leadership is that many learning leaders have no formal L&D experience. Yes, you read that right. Often, learning leaders are effective organizational managers, with many having an MBA or a project management certification. As they advance in their managerial careers, they may find themselves leading the learning and development function without fully appreciating the craft of learning experiences. While they have a good understanding of the business, they don't always have the learning and development knowledge many practitioners have. Being able to build a department that appreciates both perspectives can help with this barrier. Start small and see what progress can occur.

Another potential reason for course factories is that the department may not have the autonomy or resources to properly staff the existing workload. In a previous role, I had a team of eight, but we were never bored. In fact, each member of my team often worked on a few projects at a time to help our organization. I would also occasionally create learning experiences myself to help alleviate the burden on my team. (Plus, I didn't want them to have all the fun.) Also, while we intend to test and evaluate a learning experience, those plans can be derailed when there are constantly more learning experiences to produce. Planning and allocating resources can be tricky, especially when you have too much work and not enough people. One of the barriers I had to overcome in this role was that we also conducted new-hire orientations every week. This meant I only had access to all of my team members one day of the week, which forced me to be transparent with stakeholders about the time constraints on my team. While it didn't solve every issue, there were some stakeholders who truly understood and were flexible with us.

To further complicate matters, some learning and development departments don't have access to the people who the learning experience is designed for. I once worked in a role where I was designing for associates in a country I didn't live in. When I asked for clarity and to spend time with some of the people, I was told it wasn't possible and that I needed to produce something that could check a box confirming it was created. To design a learning experience that fits the needs of people, we need to push beyond our subject matter experts because there is often a disconnect between what they think should happen and what really happens when people do the work. To combat this barrier, remember the valuable information you can collect through a task analysis.

Despite these issues, when learning and development departments embrace UX principles, they can create a more intentional, robust learning experience, which provides content and guidance for users on how to apply it to the work that they do. While I'm not a formal UX professional, I have learned much from Don Norman, a UX pioneer and the author of the book *The Design of Everyday Things* (2013). In this book, Norman lays out multiple UX principles that can be applied to learning experience design. Let's review a few principles to guide UX and avoid becoming a learning factory pumping out ineffective training courses.

The Difference Between Human Error and Bad Design

Human error can occur for many reasons that have nothing to do with the presence of sufficient training, yet in recent years, learning and development has become a bandage for all types of organizational issues that have little to do with learning. If you look at court cases, especially about topics like sexual harassment and hostile work environments, the verdict often includes a mandate for the organization to train their staff on these topics. So, many organizations invest in learning and development for legal defensibility or compliance instead of systematically examining the sources of human error that may have contributed to the problem and actually have a chance of fixing it—for example, a breakdown in the HR complaint reporting process or a slipshod hiring practice that didn't check references thoroughly enough to recognize when a new hire had a history of harassment complaints at previous workplaces.

In this environment, how do we know if a problem is due to human error or a bad design? To begin, according to Norman, we need to consider the root cause of why something is happening. This exercise is called the "five whys," and it is a great tool for determining if a learning experience is truly needed (Figure 5-1).

Figure 5-1. Example of 5 Whys Template

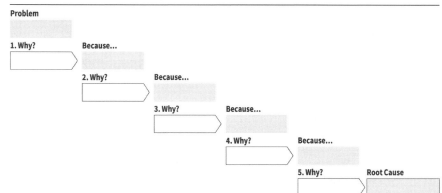

Here is an example prompt: "Imagine receiving a request for a learning experience to train IT developers at a hospital about time management because they missed a critical deadline when rolling out a new application." The first thing you should do is ask why:

1. **Why was the hospital's new healthcare app delayed by four weeks?** Answer: Additional complexities were revealed in the testing phase.
2. **Why did additional difficulties arise?** Answer: The creation phase did not include a solution for a major use case.
3. **Why did the creation phase miss a major use case?** Answer: The original brainstorming sessions did not include employees from the affected department.
4. **Why were key employees missing from the brainstorming sessions?** Answer: The brainstorming session was led by a particular department. In this case, additional departments weren't brought in until later in the development process.
5. **Why is this process managed by a particular department?** Answer: That is how it's always been done.

By going through a five whys exercise, we can determine that there were some stumbling blocks in the process for rolling out the application that had nothing to do with time management, such as not having the right people involved. Organizationally, some decisions will need to be made about how projects like this are managed in the future. In any case, the five whys revealed that building a learning experience about time management wouldn't have fixed this issue. If the learning and development department took the stakeholder at their word, they would have made something that wasted everyone's time. And then, when time management training failed to fix the issue, the stakeholder would have blamed learning design for human error.

There's one caveat that you should remember: It is impossible to fix problems that people won't admit exist. Many learning and development professionals know this all too well. Using a tool such as the five whys highlights the importance of building relationships across our organizations, not only with our subject matter experts but also our business partners, so that we can build consensus when we need backup from other departments on identifying the nontraining solutions to human error problems.

Designing for Surprises

We should focus on designing for surprises—in other words, understand that not everything will work correctly 100 percent of the time. I fully believe Murphy's Law applies to learning experiences, and I can often tell a novice learning and development professional from a seasoned one by the way they handle the unexpected. This is especially true in instructor-led training sessions. From technology snafus to people being late, it's important to be able to roll with the punches and not let emotions get the best of us.

Norman (2013) outlines five steps to consider when designing for surprises:

1. **Understand the causes of surprises and design to minimize those causes.** Why do things happen when conducting a specific task? Leverage the column of your task analysis where you ask about common errors. Are those causes comprehensive, or are there other factors involved?

2. **Do sensibility checks.** Does the action pass the "common sense" test? From the language in the task analysis to the content written for the learning experience, solicit feedback on not only the

logical order but on the appropriateness of the language for the users.

3. **Make it possible to reverse actions—or make it harder to do what cannot be reversed.** If designing an e-learning course, give people options to redo things like typing and navigating so they don't get stuck.

4. **Make it easier for people to discover the errors that do occur, and make them easier to correct.** Scenarios (which I'll discuss in chapter 7) give you a great opportunity to highlight errors and consequences.

5. **Don't treat the learner's action as an error.** Rather, try to help the person complete the action properly. Provide ways to practice applying the content to the task regardless of what goes wrong with the learning delivery.

Following these steps can smooth out the places where learning design may trip over its own feet—they lay the groundwork for a training style that is adaptive and responsive, regardless of any surprises in the design or delivery.

Designing for Everyone vs. Designing for the Average

Has anyone in your life said you are special? If not, let me tell you that you are. Learning designers are often pressured to create experiences tailored to the "average" learner. But what does it mean to be average—and does that represent a real learner or just a set of expectations shaped by culture and environment or a statistical mean that doesn't really represent any single individual? Is there a way to develop a learning experience that will work for everyone, in their own special ways, instead of designing for the average?

As there is more focus now on accessibility and universal design among many learning and development departments, paying lip service to accessibility isn't good enough anymore. I cringe when I hear "We don't have anyone here that needs any accommodations" in response to my bringing up the importance of designing a learning experience that can be used by people in different ways. First, many people have invisible disabilities that the stakeholders making the request may be unaware of. (This is a time when the shoes step can help.) Secondly, accessibility benefits everyone—it's called the curb cut effect, after it was observed that the curb cuts designed to help people in wheelchairs navigate cities were also used and appreciated by people with bikes, strollers, suitcases, and more. Finally, why wouldn't you want to create learning content that was adaptable and accessible so that users could choose to consume it in the way most likely to be effective for them?

A way to approach adaptable, accessible design for everyone is to design for interests, skills, and abilities. In my experience, learning experience designers can often forget that their products will be used by people. According to Norman (2013), this is what makes design such a rewarding discipline. I agree with that sentiment, and I frequently say that the privilege of being a part of someone's success is a position I don't take lightly.

I will discuss accessibility and global design more in the next chapter.

UI: More Than Pretty Little Next Buttons

Have you ever opened a website and thought about how well designed it was? If you enjoy the beautification of a learning experience, you probably like user interface (UI) and perhaps don't even realize it. According to Usability.gov, UI combines concepts from interaction design, visual design, and information architecture. From a UI perspective, everything we create is seen by the user. Much like the saying "We eat with our eyes" means the visual appeal of a meal is important, our learning experiences are brain food for our users. When the UI is out of touch with modern standards or is difficult for the user, it is a recipe for losing trust quickly.

Patrick Jordan explores the human elements of products in his book *Designing Pleasurable Products* (2000). One key takeaway is how *pleasure* is defined: "If a task can be accomplished with a reasonable degree of efficiency and within acceptable levels of comfort, then the product can be seen as fitting to the user." Isn't our goal to apply that concept to learning experiences? Learning experiences that are efficient keep development and time costs down. Learning experiences that are comfortable simplify the user's experience. What this doesn't account for, however, is the goals of the learning experience, which should refer back to the performance gap we are trying to solve with our learning experience.

How Does UI Affect Learning Experiences?

Jakob Neilsen, a UI pioneer, developed 10 usability heuristics. While originally created for interaction design, which is the design of products to enable a user to achieve objectives, these heuristics can also be applied to learning experience design. Let's review each.

1. Visibility of System Status

Visibility of system status is about transparency through information and feedback. Consider some examples outside learning experiences:

- The indicator on your phone for the amount of remaining battery life is represented with a visual depiction and percentage.
- A notification in a messaging app lets you know how many unread messages you have.
- A checkmark you click on a website confirms your selection when ordering a meal online.

Visibility lets us know what to expect in the system, and it responds to us as things change. Nielsen argues visibility is critical for systems to keep users informed as people strive for predictability and control. Taking this idea into consideration, it's about people having something work as expected.

A team I previously managed created a learning experience using Articulate Rise that allowed the user to select a branching path depending on their role in the company, which provided the content and specific tasks for that role along with a formative and summative assessment. My team focused so much on content development that when we rolled the product out, we felt confident it would go well. While the content and tasks were excellent, I'll never forget the angry email we received asking us for help because the learning experience was "broken." When we reached out to the user to ask for clarification about the problem, we found out that they didn't know how to scroll down so they couldn't find the next button. While our initial reaction was purely confusion as to why someone didn't know how to scroll, when considering visibility of system status, their problem made sense. This was the user's first experience with Articulate Rise, and we hadn't provided on-screen tips for them to track their progress or navigate.

There are many ways this principle can apply to our learning experiences. First, provide some way to track progress. If a user has something they need to attend to, they can estimate how much time they have left to complete. Also, make sure any interactions respond in some way to the user. For example, if you have a tile interaction, consider adding a gradient to show which tiles have been selected or consider providing a checkmark indicator. Keeping the user informed of their current status and valuing their time is critical.

2. Match Your Product With Real-World Needs and Constraints

Have you ever had trouble following a learning experience because it included too much information or too many asides? I know I have been on the receiving end of this type of confusing delivery many times. This principle challenges designers to consider what the user goes through. In the previous chapter, I discussed the role of empathy but also cautioned that empathy should align to performance tasks. The way you create learning experiences should focus on the needs of the users. What do they need to do to be successful in their jobs with the content you are providing in a learning experience?

A leader I worked with in a previous role used a method he called the Paulina Test: Before anything he created went live, he reached out to his colleague Paulina, who worked in another part of the business, and asked her to look it over. Was Paulina a subject matter expert of the organization? No. Quite the opposite, Paulina had no information about the topic. If the content was developed in such a way that Paulina could follow it, he knew he had created a good learning experience. While this test can be difficult to apply to highly technical content, it can be done. I remember developing learning experience content about troubleshooting Wi-Fi on a popular reading device that had to be something our partners in India and the Philippines could understand as well as those whose primary language was English. To make the content easy to understand, I was careful about my own language choices, defining complex terms and keeping the content as concise as possible with opportunities to deep dive if more support was needed.

For our learning experiences, we should assume nothing when it comes to words or concepts. If you use acronyms, spell them out the first time you mention them. If the content is building on a concept, consider providing a quick overview of that concept before diving in so anyone who needs a refresher can start with a similar understanding. If you can, provide some performance support to them to help reinforce the concept. User research can be vital to understand what term users are familiar with. When I worked in manufacturing, we would have specifications to 0.0001 of a unit. When talking to people who worked with our product and machines, they called this "tenths," and for the longest time, I couldn't understand why I wasn't making the connection to the numbers I was actually seeing. Instead of telling them they were wrong, we made sure to let folks know during onboarding that "tenths" at the organization was short for "ten-thousandths" and created an activity around shop mathematics to reinforce it.

3. User Control and Freedom

Have you ever made an accidental click on a website and unintentionally purchased something? What about accidentally leaving a website and going somewhere you didn't intend? I know I often experience mishaps with my Apple mouse, despite regularly using it. We've all been there, and these blunders should be considered from an UI perspective. Users can be distracted or in a hurry and make a mistake that they need to amend immediately. I've received notifications of systems blocking things that I need to interact with and of timing out on a learning experience. We want people to feel empowered and comfortable, not frustrated.

One thing that was important to me when building a learning strategy in my manufacturing role was evaluation data. I not only wanted there to be a feedback mechanism on the effectiveness and confidence of the learning experience, but I also wanted to provide some customer success or voice of the customer metrics to learn what people liked and didn't like. The organization didn't have any survey-specific software, and the way the learning management system was set up didn't allow for evaluations, so I encouraged the team to embed a feedback form into the learning experience and to have it be part of the shutdown process of the day for instructor-led training sessions. The first version of that form was set up poorly; it only let users rate one time, but it didn't allow for corrections. I didn't realize this until I got feedback from users, so—because of this mistake—I left them frustrated and in a position that did not allow them to give feedback easily.

Our learning experiences should have systems in place to help safeguard users from feeling stuck and frustrated. When possible, consider undo or redo options for digital learning experiences. If someone messes up a handout or booklet during an instructor-led training session, have backups available. In virtual instructor-led learning experiences, consider an option to erase messages quickly if someone accidentally types something private in a group setting. We want our users to feel safe, not embarrassed.

4. Consistency and Standards

Do you want to know why so many people go to YouTube or Google when they need help with something? Often, it is quicker due to the sophisticated back-end data that is optimized for searching, which is not part of many learning and development systems. I never jump over to the LMS to search for the newest learning experience, and that is likely true for you as well. Jakob's Law of Internet UX states that people spend most of their time using products other than yours. These interactions will set their expectations for what to look for in your learning experience. Beyond digital experiences, think about other examples such as hotel check-in desks (which are often located near the entrance), handicapped parking spots (which are marked with the same blue and white color scheme and a sign), and the order of buttons on a gas pump (which are listed as 87, 91, and 93). This consistency helps reduce a person's cognitive load—the mental effort required to learn new information—by forcing them to learn something new or adjust to something out of the ordinary order they are used to.

Switching jobs can be difficult for folks because organizations vary how they onboard, communicate job expectations, and even layout buildings. The same can be true for the learning technologies we use to build learning experiences. When I worked in higher education, while each online course had a similar starter shell, there was no uniformity in how the menu looked from course to course. Despite our best efforts across the university, with even the students rallying for consistency, the initiative received backlash from some faculty. Students also used end of course surveys to share their displeasure toward courses that didn't conform to a consistent structure. Unfortunately, there was little consequence for the professors, and the damage had already been done—it was harder on the student to find and access information needed in the course for them to be successful.

This doesn't mean learning experiences always need to have a company logo on them, but we should consider how to create internal uniformity in a family of products. These design systems can include but aren't limited to a style guide for guidance about putting together a learning experience, a pattern library for uniform icons across training programs, and a component library for uniform composition of the learning experiences. Additionally, we should also consider external expectations. YouTube videos have progress bars that allow you to fast forward and go back quickly. Consider adding this functionality to your videos so your user can interact with them in a familiar way.

5. Error Prevention

When I visited the Grand Canyon with my partner in 2016, we went to the western side of the natural wonder. As we walked toward the edge, a gust of wind almost knocked me down, and my Carolina Panthers hat almost blew off my head. Instinctively, I leaned forward to adjust it back down tightly to my head as my partner pulled on the back of my shirt. As soon as I looked around, I realized I was dangerously close to the edge of the canyon. I was so focused on not losing my favorite hat I had no idea how close I was to peril. Instead of immediately admitting my error, my first reaction was to ask where the guardrails were.

The same is true for our users. While a good error message can be helpful, we want to strive to prevent problems from happening in the first place. This heuristic says there are two types of errors: *slips* and *mistakes*. A slip is an unconscious error caused by inattention while a mistake is a conscious error based on a mismatch between the user's mental model and the design. So, ponder this: If I fell into the Grand Canyon, how would you classify my error? As a slip or a mistake?

From a learning design perspective, consider how slips and mistakes can happen. Slips often are made by folks with expertise who go into autopilot while doing a task. Examples on the job can include not attaching a file to an email or missing an embarrassing typo. On the other hand, mistakes happen when there is a mismatch in the skill set or mental model. Mistakes can happen due to overconfidence. Overconfidence can come from someone's tenure in an organization or from someone who thinks they know how to properly execute a task even though they haven't done it in a while. Preventing mistakes calls on us to get to know our users better and understand their expectations. Research your users; we want them to be successful in our learning experiences and be able to apply the content back to their jobs.

6. Recognition Rather Than Recall

What should users know and what is something they can retrieve later? This is a loaded question and something that a lot of folks are talking about in the learning and development space. Striving for a balance when it comes to content and application is critical. As humans, we have limited short-term memories; our working memory holds information relevant to the current task. In other words, consider human working memory as a whiteboard on which the mind records accessible information needed to execute steps in a process. If a task requires too much information, the limited capacity of our working memory can make it harder to do the task and may make it easier to commit an error.

For learning experiences that have lots of complex content to digest, when possible, consider ways to lighten this load. Providing additional performance support and just enough content to execute the task can help. I also encourage you to explore different modalities of learning experiences and include a follow-up discussion with users afterward. Reduce the amount of information that users need to remember.

7. Flexibility and Efficiency of Use

Have you ever gone through a learning experience and felt like you knew everything and it was a waste of your time? I'm sure we all have. This may happen because someone told us to create the learning experience or it was provided to fulfill a compliance or legal requirement. It doesn't mean that "spray and prays" (learning experiences that are the same for every-one) should never be used. They happen for a variety of reasons including a lower administrative burden and reduced creation time. But remember, there is a human on the other side of the learning experience. Instead of creating that one-size-fits-all content, consider how you can provide users with flexible processes in their learning experiences.

Novice and expert users have different needs. New users often need additional guidance in systems that they haven't used before. This can include wizards that guide users through a decision tree, a tutorial, or a gif demonstrating how to use something. Experts don't need this guidance and can skip over it. I'm not a fan of mandatory interface tutorials for that reason, especially if it's the first thing someone experiences. Interface tutorials are likely an engagement killer for the people who already know how to use the system.

For learning experience design, consider user autonomy and allow them to speed up and slow down as needed. Do everything you can to prevent locked navigation. Build learning experiences in a way that allows for user shortcut keys. Separate what can be off-loaded into a resource guide as performance support on the back end of the learning experience.

8. Aesthetic and Minimalist Design

Have you ever heard of the acronym KISS—*keep it simple silly*? (I'm not a fan of calling anyone *stupid*.) Simple and clean does not mean easy. In fact, it can be extremely difficult to design this for simplicity, especially when you have overenthusiastic stakeholders demanding more pictures and information. It doesn't mean you have to be boring either. Simplicity means that the visual elements support the user's primary goals in the learning experience. Don't let anything unnecessary distract the users from the information they need. I remember a class I took online in graduate school that used an ugly stock image of a person in overalls giving a thumbs up, and I was so fixated on why that was a design choice and the message it was trying to convey—I couldn't tell you much about the content in the course, but I still remember that picture vividly.

For learning experiences, let the content and the tasks guide your development. Not colors. Not a great music beat. Not the cute gif that is your favorite of the week. Remember, you are not the user. Keep it simple, and focus on what they need to be successful in the roles they were hired to do.

9. Help Users Recover From Errors

Have you ever just felt stuck using something? I've felt that way using various learning technologies, but I've also felt that way in learning experiences. Think about a "wrong way" road sign. Its function is simple, and you can only see it if you are headed in the wrong direction. When there is a problem or an error, give users ways to recognize it, diagnose the problem, and recover. Feedback should be targeted, language should be plain and understandable, and there should be a specific call to action so they know what to do next.

One of my biggest pet peeves is when an assessment won't allow you to continue if you select an incorrect answer but gives you absolutely no feedback on how to correct course. It's like you are trapped in some horrible twilight zone, and your user may completely check-out afterward. I like to have folks try an assessment twice and then allow them to keep moving. There are ways you can nudge them later to help build mastery in learning technology systems, such as through Axonify.

10. Help and Documentation

If you have to overexplain something, there is a good chance it is poorly designed. You may need to provide documentation and help with using a system to complete tasks, but the burden of figuring out how to access, navigate, or use a learning experience should not be on the user. When I changed jobs one time, my new company relied on a payroll system I hadn't used before. I found it frustrating when I tried to request time off. I couldn't use the web version, so I downloaded the app on my phone because it had a shortcut to request time off. I was motivated to take time off, so I was determined to do whatever I could to make it happen. Our users won't feel the same way about our learning experiences.

When creating help documentation, remember these tips:

- Make it is easy to access, and provide headings and anchor links if possible to help the user quickly find the content they are looking for.
- Ask for feedback by adding a link to a form or an email address. That way users can inform you if something is not up to date or needs more clarification. After all, things can change quickly, and even the most diligent designers can forget something.
- Anchor the content around what someone needs know (a task perspective).

Conclusion

Combining elements of UX (user experience) and UI (user interface) into our learning experience design process is critical for designing the best products possible. Through UX, we want to improve the whole experience for people and be mindful of the design of everything from how they access the content to where it lives. Through UI, on the other hand, we focus on improving presentation, including the look, feel, and content. Is it clear to users what they should be doing, or does your learning experience leave people confused?

Up next, we'll explore accessibility and how we need to make learning experiences that can be used by everyone.

30/60/90 Plan

Consider different elements of this chapter, and use the 30/60/90 plan template as a starter; better yet, tailor one to where you are on the journey.

30 days: Select a UX or UI aspect you'd like to start incorporating in your work.

60 days: Incorporate the aspect in your design process and ask for feedback from users and team members.

90 days: Iterate and reflect on what has worked and what hasn't.

Chapter 6
The Product: Accessibility

In this chapter, we will explore:

◉ Using the acronym POUR to create accessible learning experiences

◉ Understanding global and technical considerations in designing learning experiences

There is something that I've been embarrassed by for a while and often hide in public. For the past few years, I've struggled to hear well. The worst times are those when there is additional noise in the background, like loud music or talking. I used to just smile and nod when someone spoke to me if I couldn't hear them, but I've become more comfortable telling people that I'm hard of hearing and may need them to repeat something in a loud environment. Additionally, my partner was born Deaf in one ear, so as I've struggled with hearing loss, he's shared some tips to make social settings better. Beyond social settings, my ability to hear in professional settings has also given me anxiety, especially when a conference speaker forwent using a microphone because their "voice carries."

Then in October 2018, I read an article someone shared on Twitter about Google Slides introducing a feature that used artificial intelligence (AI) to generate captions to display under the slide show in real time. I was preparing to debut a presentation about learner engagement at the Association for Education Communication and Technology (AECT) conference, and I decided to go for it and use the new feature there. While my room initially didn't have that many attendees, people were encouraging others to come in to witness the marvel of live AI captioning. Since that moment, I've incorporated live AI captioning in all my presentations because it takes two clicks for me to do, helps me focus on my words better while presenting, and most importantly, allows other people to more easily enjoy my content.

Why Accessibility?

While I'm certainly not perfect, I've tried my best to be an advocate for accessibility and inclusion in my design process. My friend Nick Tillem went viral on Twitter in 2022 for saying this better than I could: "Accessibility isn't extra steps, it's steps you've missed." There are many reasons beyond my personal connection that I think it is necessary for us to be advocates for accessibility and inclusion, but I'll share some of the most important ones:

- **We serve people.** You may be sick of me saying how critical it is that we serve people, but we do. People have different needs, and we may not know what our learners need. Designing our learning experiences to be accessible is a way to reach all learners.

- **It saves time and money.** There is a myth that it takes too long to create accessible learning experiences. I believe this came from organizations that had to retrofit existing learning experiences to make parts of them accessible by adding a transcript or captions, changing the medium, or adding tab order and alternative text to e-learning courses. I've found that once accessibility is part of your design process from the beginning, you can plan ahead better while scoping a project, so it actually becomes harder not to accommodate.

- **It's the right thing to do.** Like the example I shared of my avoiding presentations with a speaker who forgoes using a mic, even if there are no bad intentions meant by the speaker, their lack of consideration for accessibility makes it difficult to focus at best and can make me feel like I don't matter at worst.

An argument I've heard often about ignoring the need to make learning experiences more accessible and inclusive is that the user population doesn't have anyone who needs accommodations. That's a dangerous assumption for several reasons. We shouldn't assume someone who needs an accommodation will self-identify. In conference sessions where I can't hear, I'm not going to stand up and disrupt the session. Maybe some people would, but that's not me, as I don't want to put more attention on myself. Also, creating accessible learning experiences may fulfill needs for those who may need temporary accommodations, which are not always considered. For example, someone who doesn't have headphones to watch a video or someone holding a baby while working from home—they can't use a mouse, but they may be able to use the arrow keys on the keyboard. Following accessible learning design principles benefits everyone.

When some people start designing learning experiences, they may use their current training population or personas to guide their design choices. Often, personas include personal identifiers like ability, race, economic status, language, age, and gender, but you can also account for disabilities that are permanent, temporary, or situational in your designs. Someone with a permanent disability might have permanent loss of hearing, sight, or smell. Someone else might have a temporary impairment, like a broken arm or loss of hearing after a loud concert.

We also need to be mindful of situational challenges. Situational challenges often aren't considered legal disabilities, but we still need to account for them. For example, a situational challenge occurs when you work in a loud environment and may not be able to reply to verbal cues in a video. If someone is watching a training video while working from home, they may need to step away from the learning experience; the course should allow pausing to accommodate the situational challenge.

While accessibility could be its own book, I decided to focus here on the POUR acronym to provide context on elements that should be adhered to in accessible LXD. This chapter won't provide every consideration for accessibility, but I hope it serves as a starting point and encourages you to explore more resources.

POUR

When thinking about accessibility, many learning experience designers can become overwhelmed with knowing where to start and what should or should not be included when creating accessible learning experiences. The National Center on Accessible Educational Materials (2022) created an acronym—POUR—that helps define four qualities of an accessible learning experience: perceivable, operable, understandable, and robust. Let's explore each of these qualities to deconstruct what this means for our learning experiences.

Perceivable

According to the National Center on Accessible Educational Materials, *perceivable* means ensuring your training population can experience your content. To optimize your learning experiences to be more perceivable to your training population, learning experience designers should add alternative text, use captioning and transcripts, use colors with high contrast, and make text readable.

Alternative Text

Alternative text (or alt text) for images is a necessary component of creating an accessible learning experience. While it can be a feature that is easy to implement, it can also be a challenge to create a suitable alternative text for complex images. Alt text provides a text alternative to nontext content and can affect e-learning modules, videos, and even print documents. Alternative text has many functions:

- It is read by screen readers in place of images, allowing the content and function of the image to be accessible to those with visual or certain cognitive disabilities.
- In browsers, it is displayed in place of the image if the image file doesn't load due to errors or bandwidth issues or if the user has chosen not to view images.
- It provides a semantic meaning and description to images, which can be read by search engines or be used to later determine the content of the image from page context alone.

Furthermore, the Web Accessibility in Mind organization states that text must be provided to the end user, which presents the content and function of images within your learning content. The *content* is the composition of the image and the *function* is why the image is being used. If you can't describe the function of an image, it's a good indication you may want to remove it entirely. Here are some other considerations about how to decide which elements of an image are needed to understand the content:

- Is the image part of an introduction for a chapter or lesson? How does this text relate to the rest of the material? If it's not teaching a concept it may not need to be described in detail.
- Is the image the central point of a lesson? In other words, is this critical to understanding the content? If so, it is a critical part of the learning concept and should it be described as thoroughly as possible.
- Is the image purely decorative? For example, is it the facilitator's headshot or the organization's logo? If it does not teach anything, describe it as a decorative image and avoid sharing irrelevant information.
- Is the image part of an assessment or activity? If so, be sure to describe the specific pieces of information needed to complete the task. Be sure not to give away the answer in the alt-text, so consider how you write your assessment or activity and ensure the image description doesn't tell the answer.

Style and Language of Alt Text

Context is key when it comes to writing alt text, so descriptions for the same image may differ depending on the context. The first thing you should do when creating alt text is to consider what the image is saying regarding the content. Is it an illustrative element showing something that has already been explained in the text, or is the image essential to understanding the concept?

Let's pretend you are asked to provide alt text for a portrait of Alexander Hamilton. The way you create alt text for this portrait will differ greatly depending on the content in the learning experience. If you are describing his career and provide this image as a focal point in the learning experience, acceptable alt text would be simple: *Portrait of Alexander Hamilton.*

However, if you were adding this picture to a discussion about the fashion of US presidents, the acceptable alt text may be something more extensive: *Portrait of Alexander Hamilton wearing a black double-breasted wool coat with a white silk ruffle shirt.*

Captioning and Transcripts

Captions allow users who are Deaf or hard of hearing to experience content to its fullest extent. Additionally, captions and transcripts allow folks who want to skim content afterward to have access to the full content. Captions can also help if someone doesn't have a set of headphones to listen with or if they have trouble understanding the speaker. There are also, depending on where the information is hosted, options for users to select captions in their preferred language, which can help with comprehension. I've been using live AI-generated captions for presentations through Google Slides, but this feature is now available across other presentation programs as well as virtual communication software such as Microsoft Teams and Zoom.

When creating captions and transcripts, accuracy is key. Captions should be synchronized and delivered at the same time audio is being heard. Additionally, according to the Federal Communications Commission (2021), captions should not only match spoken words but also convey background noises and other sounds to the fullest degree possible. This may even include indicating periods of silence, so people using the captions don't wonder if they're missing something during long breaks in speaking. If you'd like more guidance on captioning, I encourage you to search for audio description videos, of which you can find many examples via YouTube and even Netflix.

To generate transcripts, I encourage you to create PDFs that users can download to read in full. In e-learning authoring tools, you often can build in a notes or resources tab to provide access to the transcript. Also, consider the use of color and contrast in your designs as well as your transcripts, and be mindful of font choices and size for readability.

Reflection: Take a moment to reflect on *perceivable* priniciples of accessibility, and make some notes on ways you can apply them to your own design process.

Now that we've covered the elements that make your content perceivable, let's move on to the other parts of POUR: operable, understandable, and robust.

Operable

Operable means ensuring people can interact with your content using a variety of tools. To fulfill the purpose of the techniques under the operable umbrella, you need to create headings, descriptive links, and keyboard accessibility.

Create Headings

Headings act as landmarks for assistive technology such as screen readers, and they assist with the overall readability of the learning experience. By selecting a heading from a list, users can skip ahead to specific sections. This capability of screen readers significantly improves the user experience and the efficiency with which users with visual impairments can navigate long experiences. For this to work, make sure the headings are in the correct order and nested.

Create Descriptive Links

Creating descriptive links can give people using keyboard shortcuts a better understanding of the content. Specifically, to create more accessible learning experiences, avoid link language such as "click here" or "learn more." Keep in mind that providing the full URL address can also be confusing for users. If a user is going through your learning experience using a screen reader, it will read aloud the full URL. Ideally, links should describe the content they reference as much as possible. For example, "Click here to read the full code of ethics" or "Click this link to visit the manufacturer's site for customer service requests."

Create Keyboard Accessibility

Much of the work of ensuring keyboard accessibility involves a deep understanding of the specific technology tools you are using to create e-learning content or videos. Nevertheless, learning experience designers are increasingly involved in creating content that remixes already existing resources, including interactive widgets and forms. At minimum, you should know how to test for keyboard accessibility so that when you add keyboard shortcuts to your content you are not creating barriers for users.

The test for keyboard accessibility begins with a simple keyboard shortcut: Pressing Tab will allow you to navigate the interactive elements (form fields or hyperlinks). Pressing Shift and Tab together will allow you to navigate in the opposite direction. As you navigate using the keyboard, it should be clear which element is in focus (as indicated by a border or other styling). Also, you should make sure that the focus moves around the content in a logical manner.

If keyboard accessibility is not supported, you should consider a different resource that provides equivalent access to the information for those who require alternative input methods. When building digital learning experiences in e-learning authoring tools, you can set what is called "tab order" to improve keyboard accessibility. This allows a user experiencing your content with assistive technology better navigate through the learning experience.

Reflection: Take a moment to reflect on *operable* principles of accessibility, and make some notes on ways you can apply them to your own design process.

Understandable

Understandable means ensuring people can understand your content and enjoy a consistent learning experience. In this section, we will explore writing in plain language, inclusive language, and language identified for screen readers.

Plain Language

Because so much content provided to us is technical and specific to the organizations we serve, learning professionals sometimes overlook how it is written. Additionally, people who have different cognitive needs or learning disabilities may struggle to understand training material. Writing in plain language can benefit anyone. Organizations can also help by providing content in a logical order, which aids readability. Furthermore, check your writing for any abbreviations or language that people may not know. When I worked at Amazon, I was introduced to a tool called the Gunning Fog Index, which scans content to provide an overall reading level. Many word processing programs such as Microsoft Word and Google Docs provide this information too.

Inclusive Language

The learning experiences we create and manage can go to anyone in the organization. Therefore, we have an obligation to be inclusive in our learning experiences, so we should take care when choosing the language we use.

Everyone wins when language is respectful and inclusive. A tool I like using to add clarity around this is Alex.js. It is a free AI tool that scans your text for words and phrases that may not be as inclusive. Like most tools, it isn't perfect; however, it can provide a great audit for when you're writing content.

Some of the best advice around inclusive language is knowing that language is always changing. It's imperative that we lean into being lifelong learners and seek to understand specific meanings of words. Furthermore, we should seek clarity around how groups self-identify to ensure proper terminology.

Finally, if we make a mistake around language, we should use that as an opportunity to learn and grow. The work that we do can affect everyone in our organizations; even if we don't think about it in this way, we are often "the face" of an organization, through someone's first experience in onboarding or compliance training. When mistakes are made, acknowledge them, be accountable, and seek to rectify in the future.

Language for Screen Readers

Screen readers often support multiple languages, making them powerful tools for folks who use them. They are limited, however, because the language of your experience needs to be defined for them to function properly for their users. TD professionals need to accurately identify the language of their learning experience so that screen readers can work appropriately.

Reflection: Take a moment to reflect on *understandable* principles of accessibility, and make some notes on ways you can apply them to your own design process.

Robust

According to the National Center on Accessible Educational Materials, *robust* means ensuring your content works well within current and future technologies. In this section, we will explore descriptive metadata and testing for accessibility.

Provide Descriptive Metadata

Metadata is data or information about other data. Some examples include the date a learning experience was created and the title of the learning experience. By tagging metadata and providing it, you can help a screen reader determine what information is in the learning experience. As previously mentioned, titles and headers are a great start. Additionally, identifying metadata can help you appropriately tag the content in the various systems used by the organization, such as a knowledge management system or an LMS.

Conduct Accessibility Tests

You should also test what you create for accessibility and platform viability. There are many tools that can assist you. Regardless of whether you use a Mac or PC, screen readers are available for free. Additionally, test what you create on multiple browsers and platforms to see if your learning experience functions appropriately. It's always a good use of time to conduct accessibility audits using assistive technology, but it's even better if you can leverage testers who use these technologies to provide a snapshot of what it is like going through materials and needing the assistive technologies to use the product.

Reflection: Take a moment to reflect on *robust* principles of accessibility, and make some notes on ways you can apply them to your own design process.

WCAG

The Web Content Accessibility Guidelines (WCAG) is a collaborative effort with the goal of providing a single shared standard for web content accessibility that meets the needs of all. These guidelines, while often tailored to web development, are useful for those who create learning experiences using various learning technologies.

Remember POUR? Let's explore those techniques in relation to the WCAG (Table 6-1).

Table 6-1. Mapping POUR to WCAG

LXD Action	Related WCAG
Perceivable	
If on camera (in virtual instructor-led or recorded video), use good lighting	1.4.8 Visual Presentation
Create a transcript of the session	1.2.2 Captions
Offer handouts and other materials ahead of time	1.4.8 Visual Presentation; 1.2.2 Captions
Caption audio or make it available	1.2.2 Captions
Use high color contrast and don't use only color to distinguish function or mood	1.4.3 Contrast Minimum
Use descriptive alternative text that focuses on content and function	1.1.1 Nontext Content

Table 6-1. (cont.)

LXD Action	Related WCAG
Operable	
Set slide or tab order	2.1.1 Keyboard; 2.1.2 No Keyboard Trap
Title each slide (header) and use clear structure	2.4.1 Bypass Blocks; 2.4.6 Headings and Labels
Segment recordings by topic and timestamp	2.4.6 Headings and Labels
Schedule breaks for participant needs (for virtual instructor-led, hybrid, and in-person)	2.2.1 Timing Adjustable
Remove timed assessments and "time out" for non-mouse movement	2.2.1 Timing Adjustable
Create descriptive links that share context	2.4.4 Link Purpose
Understandable	
Keep motion/animation minimal	1.3.3 Sensory Characteristics
Limit text on slide	3.3.2 Labels and Instructions
Speak clearly into microphone (voice over, hybrid, in-person, and virtual instructor-led)	3.1.5 Reading Level
Define abbreviations first before using	3.1.4 Abbreviations; 3.1.3 Unfamiliar Words
Audit content for language and reading level	3.1.5 Reading Level
Create descriptive links that share context	2.4.4 Link Purpose
Robust	
Ask for feedback on materials	Cumulative
Check materials in gray scale	Cumulative
Check accessibility as you create	Cumulative
Test outside software (if used) for accessibility	Cumulative

Some considerations can feed into all four areas of POUR; these may include global inclusion and accessibility and technical considerations. Let's explore these a little closer.

Global Accessibility

If the COVID-19 pandemic has taught us anything, it is that we are all in this together and many organizations now consider themselves global. Even if your organization isn't considered global, as a learning experience designer you are a global citizen when you create learning experiences. What exactly is global accessibility? And what does it have to do with design? No two users are exactly alike. Physical and cognitive disabilities as well as environmental factors (hardware, software, and beyond) can inhibit people from fully engaging with learning experiences. As learning experience designers, we often find similar issues that affect our users' ability to interact, and while the restrictions across users and use cases vary, the design implications are similar.

Living in an increasingly globalized world means that there's an opportunity to proactively build ethical and meaningful learning experiences that are inclusive of societies and cultures worldwide. Let's start that journey by learning more about designing for global accessibility. Understand that accessibility is almost always intersectional; norms of gender, religion, or class may further include or exclude people from our learning experiences.

A concern that comes up often, especially if you are contemplating this for the first time, is how to be intentional and mindful when representing users. When creating learning experiences for the majority population, learning experience designers often imagine a target user based on their familiar assumptions. We need to expand our idea of the average target user in representation choices—don't exclude people with disabilities from advancing and meaningfully using your learning experience. Remember that representation does not mean adding a token solo shot of a user with a disability, but truly aim for broader inclusion in society. One of my favorite stock art collections is called Disabled and Here. It is a disability-led stock image library that also celebrates other forms of diversity. As a bonus, the site provides alternative text for you to use with the images.

Accommodate Different Levels of Literacy and Different Languages

English is a dominant language on the web, but globally, it's not as widely spoken or understood. According to the Press Trust of India (2018), India has 22 official languages with more than a million speakers each. One of my best friends is from India, and she's explained India's languages to me as if India were like the United States—each state has its own language.

When users open your learning experience, they may rely on symbols and pictures, potentially with accessibility aids, to perform tasks, even if these aren't characters and symbols you are used to.

Here are some best practices to keep in mind when considering language:

- Use basic, simple English, and keep text jargon free. By doing so not only are you keeping the content straightforward but it helps with translation.
- Keep sentences short and concise. In addition, consider providing graphical cues to guide speakers of other languages, nonliterate users, and people with cognitive disabilities.

Ensure That Your Learning Experience Functions Seamlessly in Intermittent Networks and When Offline

Network coverage in emerging markets is often sluggish, sparse, and unpredictable; as a result, users may opt for slower speeds or turn off their mobile data manually to save money. My parents in northeastern Kentucky are lucky to get an internet speed of 1 Mbps, which is about the speed of dial-up internet service from 20 years ago. When I visit them, I often pop over whatever I need into a document that I can access offline so I can continue to work. Keep in mind that accessibility services can require additional bandwidth from the network. For example, a learning experience that is screen reader accessible—allowing the page to be read aloud for blind or visually impaired people—but fails to perform well on an intermittent network has limited utility. Here are some best practices:

- Test your learning experience in airplane mode to simulate a lack of connectivity.
- Make learning experience content available offline whenever possible.

Conclusion

People with disabilities use a variety of assistive technologies to access learning experiences. If you build your learning experience with those functions in mind, you can increase the amount of people who can use them. I recommend testing components and user flows through your learning experience regularly with a variety of assistive technologies and accessibility settings turned on. Here are some best practices to remember:

- Simulate most important use cases and scenarios with accessibility settings enabled.
- Test with real users in various countries as often as possible to gain insights for improvements.

Inclusive design and accessible learning experiences open the door for people to overcome barriers that prevent them from full participation in our workplaces. It is upon us as learning experience designers to make intentional design decisions that serve all users with disabilities in all contexts and in all countries. Access should be a key tenet for all we do.

30/60/90 Plan

As you consider how to apply the content from this chapter, please know this is a journey. Your work and mindset won't instantly become accessible and inclusive overnight. Additionally, if you are considering accessibility and inclusion, there are likely some aspects you can improve. This 30/60/90 plan gives you the opportunity for improvement, no matter where you are on your journey.

30 days: Select an accessibility component you'd like to add to your work.

60 days: Incorporate the aspect in your design process and ask for feedback from users and team members.

90 days: Iterate and reflect on what has worked and what hasn't.

Chapter 7
The Product: Assessments

In this chapter, we will explore:

⦿ Reasons to assess learning

⦿ Assessment techniques

⦿ Creating scenarios

One of the most critical parts of the learning experience design process is assessment, yet we often don't know how to appropriately assess. In this book, we'll use *assessment* to refer to how we test learners' acquisition of knowledge and skills, and *evaluation* to refer to how we judge the design and effectiveness of our learning products (chapter 10). To me, assessment is the love language of learning experience design. If it is done properly, not only are you able to provide valuable information to people that they can apply to their jobs, but you are also able to gain a clear picture of what additional support they need. From an organizational standpoint, when done right, assessments can give you accurate information about whether your learning experience hit the mark for the KPI you set. I don't think assessment is something that people intend to mess up, but I think it is something that collectively can be a struggle. Furthermore, if you ask organizations to describe the purpose of our work, you'll likely get differing answers, including legal defensibility, expanded individual and organizational capacity, increased revenue, and decreased costs.

While much of this book does focus on people, it is important to know that we wouldn't have jobs if we didn't serve our organizations in some capacity. In other words, we are meant to serve our organizations, and the people we support in our organizations are meant to produce, not just complete learning experiences. Simply, assessments should be rooted in what someone needs to do and know, and evaluation should provide evidence that tasks have been executed correctly. By adopting learning experience design principles and building a proper assessment and evaluation framework, we can serve both the people and the organization. Before we dive into this chapter, reflect on how you assess your learning experiences.

Assessments

One of the best things that ever happened in my career occurred in 2017 when I had the opportunity to work on a project to write end of course exams for the state of Ohio's Career-Technical Education courses. The program was led by a psychometrician, a practitioner in the science of measurement, who made it meaningful. Initially, I was concerned that this opportunity may be another detour on my desired career path, which was to continue climbing the talent development ladder. Instead, I learned so much about assessment working on that project that I not only became a better designer but eventually a better learning leader. I won't pretend to be a psychometrician, but allow me to walk through some of the biggest takeaways I learned.

Working With Subject Matter Experts

My role on this project was leading the item writing workshops (the workshops where we wrote the test questions), and a large part of my work involved working with subject matter experts. It was not unlike the work of designing learning experiences; however, we worked synchronously with SMEs alongside us throughout development. During the workshops, a facilitator (me or my co-workers) would go into a breakout room with a few subject matter experts. These SMEs taught secondary or postsecondary courses for the subject matter the test questions were being written for. Each breakout room was given a subset of the total questions to write; this is where it would get interesting. After swapping "war stories" about the content and how they delivered it to their students, it was often difficult for us to keep the SMEs on task while also encouraging them to write assessments that upheld psychometric best practices. Through this experience, I learned how to capture the spirit of what the subject matter expert wanted to assess and translate it on the fly into questions that were more psychometric.

The most difficult part came after the quota of questions were written when we all gathered to participate in a live quality assurance session. We displayed each question on a screen and asked the subject matter experts about the quality of the question, such as if it was accurate and if it aligned to state standards. In every group, there was at least one contrarian who, even if they had written the questions, would not like anything. For that reason, we sought group consensus on every single question. Now, because this was a large bank of questions—as opposed to the few questions in a typical learning experience—the live quality assurance process was often taxing, taking several hours and leading to spirited debates. Of course, we always had the option to throw the questions out the window, but that could only be done a few times before jeopardizing the composition of the exam. Keeping the quality assurance process moving along without cutting someone off and making sure everyone was heard were skills that I honed. I certainly wasn't perfect, and I know I upset a few SMEs along the way, but being in that high-pressure situation helped me learn how to handle heated conversations better.

Even subject matter experts need to understand their assignments clearly and what's in it for them (WIIFM), along with the purpose of the work. To align the SMEs when they go off on tangents or when they disagree about a single word choice, keep a North Star metric in mind: "How does this assess what someone needs to know or do in this course?" If this question couldn't be answered, then we wouldn't include that exam question in the assessment. A key part of learning experience design is keeping the content targeted and precise enough to give users the information, a way to apply it to their job, and the space to practice. Good assessments can help with application and practice, especially scenarios, which we will explore later in this chapter.

Writing Better Multiple-Choice Questions

We initially used a manual with a list of dos and don'ts for writing better assessments, but I knew there had to be a better way to convey the information. I found it difficult to apply the concepts, such as balancing the length of answer choices, without an example of them in practice. When learning is framed in the lens of change, the ability to adapt to new information can help people learn the information and help facilitate change (Dirksen 2015). The SMEs motivated us to write better multiple-choice questions, and this content was something non-SMEs (other teachers in the state of Ohio) could also use in their classrooms as well.

There is a primary point I want to highlight about taking this manual and transforming it into an e-learning course: Poorly written assessments don't measure content knowledge; they measure deduction skills. To give folks an opportunity to apply this in action, I wrote the content for *Multiple-Choice Mayhem*, an e-learning game with questions based on facts from Ripley's Believe It or Not. In the game, poorly written questions allowed participants to see how some questions can give away clues that prompt participants to guess the correct answers. *Multiple-Choice Mayhem* was created through funding from the Ohio Department of Education, and it is available for anyone to play. If you'd like to experience it, visit the website, go.osu.edu/sme3.

If you use multiple-choice questions in your learning experiences, here is some advice:

- **Just ask the question.** Consider removing questions like "Which of the following is a true statement?" or "Which of the following is a false statement?" These aren't questions. To answer them, people have to read all the answer choices. Also, without reading the options, people would have no idea what the topic of the question is. I'm a believer in keeping it simple and clean. Ask the question that you want answered.
- **You aren't Alex Trebek.** Do you want me to let you in on a dark secret about Jeopardy? The way the trivia prompts are written can leave context clues in the stems that can help you guess the correct answer. When I'm on a roll answering prompts

correctly, it's mostly due to the context clues. But your organization is not Jeopardy, and writing questions in this way gives you no evidence that learners acquired knowledge because someone could guess their way to a correct answer. For some industries with high stakes, that is a problem. I recommend keeping questions targeted and without clues to help people guess the correct answer.

- **Parallelism.** When writing options for a multiple-choice test item, it's common for the correct answer to have precise information. This often happens when SMEs (with the best intentions) add more context on why it should be the correct answer. Sometimes the result is the correct answer being longer than the others. You may be familiar with a common standardized test taking strategy: The longest answer is the correct answer. Don't do this when writing multiple-choice test items. Instead, try to make every answer choice a similar length.

While there are more tips and tricks about writing multiple-choice test items, these are some of the techniques you can quickly implement to make your tests more effective. I think that a well-written multiple-choice test item can assess knowledge at the recall and application levels. A litmus test of a good assessment is to ask yourself, how is this question related to what someone will do with the content? Is there a practice application where they can apply this information to understand what's in it for them and relate it back to the job they are doing? I can say that too often in my career, my assessments didn't pass this test. Not to pick on compliance training, but many compliance training programs I've seen have questions for which you can easily guess the correct answer and that offer no application to the user. They are often written at such a high level of abstraction, it's difficult to anchor the user in the content, let alone the assessment.

The Value of a Work-Based Scenario

Aside from multiple-choice exams, one of the most valuable types of assessments you can create is a scenario. A scenario is a work-based situation that allows users to practice the task or apply the content they've learned. It's a

great way to allow participants to experiment and try without any consequences on the job. According to Clark (2012), scenario-based e-learning
is a "preplanned guided inductive learning environment designed to accel-
erate expertise in which the learner assumes the role of an actor respond-
ing to a work-realistic assignment or challenge, which in turn responds to
reflect the learner's choices."

My own definition of scenarios contrasts with Clark's in one distinct
way: Through my work on assessment, I've found it best to anchor the user
in a realistic but straightforward experience. Too often, I've read scenarios
that I call "reality shows," which are complex and needlessly hard to follow. Consider this complicated example:

> Carlos is an early childhood education center manager. He is out of
> the office, and his direct report Marlowe is running the center today.
> At the end of the day, Alyssa, a student of the center, is waiting to be
> picked up. The phone rings and it is Rudy, Alyssa's uncle, who asks
> if Alyssa can be picked up by their neighbor Charlotte. According to
> state privacy laws, what should Marlowe tell Rudy?

The scenario has too much backstory and quite the cast of characters.
The assessment question isn't a bad one if this was part of a learning experience about early childhood education and laws. But who is the test taker
in the scenario? A fundamental problem here is that they aren't Marlowe.
They have no clue if Marlowe is someone who follows procedures or if he
does whatever he wants. Therefore, I am a proponent of anchoring the
learner in the scenario. Consider this rewrite:

> You are an early childhood education center manager. At the end of
> the day, a student of the center is waiting to be picked up. The phone
> rings, and it is someone who identifies himself as the student's uncle
> asking if the student can be picked up by their neighbor. According to
> state privacy laws, what should you tell the caller?

This example is simplified but doesn't lose any of the necessary context. Now, it's clear who the learner is in the scenario and what they're

expected to know. By simplifying, you make the scenario less about reading comprehension (which requires learners to decipher a bunch of unnecessary names, roles, and responsibilities) and more like a straightforward work example that the test taker can answer.

There are other components of scenarios that should be explored including alignment, feedback, and consequences. If the scenario has no alignment to the key performance indicators of the learning experience, get rid of it. Instead, make sure that practice is the primary purpose of your scenarios. Michael Allen (2020) says, "When it is time to perform that's not the time to practice." People don't just want performance criteria when they take a training course; they want to get a clear picture of what their job entails. We can provide alternatives to "flying by the seat of your pants" on the job through our development of robust work-based scenarios. If you decide to do a task analysis like I mentioned in chapters 4 and 5, the great news is you have a wealth of information to pull from to build meaningful task-centered scenarios.

Additionally, be deliberate with the type of feedback learners will receive for correct and incorrect choices. Go beyond saying "good job" or "that's wrong." When possible, add in some real-life consequences to make it more realistic. At a minimum, I recommend feedback provide two criteria: an explanation for correct answers and reasons with evidence for incorrect answers.

Tom Kuhlmann (2009) created a model called 3C—challenge, choices, and consequences—to help build interactive scenarios. Is there a dealbreaker, or something that the user absolutely must master before continuing? If there is, the consequence for answering that question incorrectly could be going back to the content or providing more content to help the user gain clarity about the topic.

Scenario-Based Learning Domains

The work of Ruth Colvin Clark (2012) provides eight different scenario learning domains for learning experiences: soft or interpersonal skills; legal requirements or compliance policies and procedures; troubleshooting; research and application; tradeoffs or risk management; operations decisions and tasks; development and design; and planning or resource management. Let's explore them more in depth.

Soft or Interpersonal Skills

A typical request for many talent development professionals is to provide soft skills training. There are many flavors of this request from leadership training for seasoned and new leaders to interpersonal skills training. For this learning domain, Clark (2012) states that the desired outcome is to communicate effectively to achieve organizational goals. Here's an example scenario:

> You are a customer service associate who takes customer escalations. You are speaking to a customer who says your company sent the wrong item. The customer ordered the new video game system but received a previous generation. The customer says this was a gift for a loved one and that your company ruined the occasion. You look at the available inventory, and you see that the item is out of stock, with no information as to when it will be back in stock. The customer insists if you don't make it right, they will share their poor experience on social media.
>
> Possible questions for this domain include:
> - What are some ways you can communicate that the desired item is out of stock to the customer in a way that will de-escalate the situation?
> - Because the item is out of stock, what are some alternatives you could offer the customer?

Legal Requirements or Compliance Policies and Procedures

The domain for learning legal requirements or compliance policies and procedures is usually classified as compliance training. Some examples include ethics training and sexual harassment and reporting training. Compliance training also upholds quality policies and procedures in many environments, especially (in my experience) in manufacturing. This type of training must be provided to earn various credentials and for proof of those credentials during audits. According to Clark (2012), a good way to build a scenario for this type of training is to question learners on actions that directly involve legal and organizational policy guidelines. Here's an example scenario:

> You are a housing director at a university, and you have received multiple calls from guardians of students complaining about a particular student housing complex. Some are upset about an uptick in property theft, while others complain about the deterioration of the building, making claims of unsafe habitation environments due to the presence of mold. When you reach out to the property director, they assure you that they have handled the problems, but you want to see the property yourself. You are hyperaware of various political repercussions that could affect your boss, the legal partner of the property director. Additionally, you are bound by certain laws such as the right to fair housing, implied warranty of habitability, and privacy rights.
>
> Possible questions for this scenario include:
> - ▶ According to the implied warranty of habitability statute, what actions should you take?
> - ▶ What are some considerations in this scenario regarding the right to fair housing?
> - ▶ Do you have the authority to visit the residence after the property director assures you that it is under control?

Troubleshooting

While not exclusive to these industries, troubleshooting scenarios could be great for software as a service (SaaS) or manufacturing settings. Some training topics could include diagnosing an issue, interpreting an error message, or walking a customer through a troubleshooting wizard. According to Clark (2012), a helpful troubleshooting scenario would be one in which learners must diagnose a problem and determine the next steps. Here's an example scenario:

> You are a customer service agent who is helping a customer with an issue with their tablet. They call you and say that their home Wi-Fi will not connect. They also tried connecting to a public hot spot at their local coffee shop. You

pull up the customer's information and see this is their third replacement device in a year, so you are suspicious about their claims.

Possible questions for this scenario include:

- ▶ According to our replacement and warranty policies, how would you determine whether the customer is eligible for a replacement?
- ▶ What additional information would you ask the customer to better inform your decision?
- ▶ What are some other actions you could tell the customer to try with their tablet to determine why the Wi-Fi signal won't connect?

Research and Application

There are many different industries that could benefit from scenarios grounded in research and application. Some training examples could include reading and interpreting a legal document or applying a new policy to an old product. According to Clark (2012), the purpose of this type of scenario is to assess how well learners identify and assess data sources and make decisions and recommendations based on information. Here's an example scenario:

You are a healthcare provider, and your patient is in the office for a follow-up appointment. She is asking you to consider writing a stronger prescription for her asthma. When going over her answers to the asthma survey and management chart, you see the following information:

Asthma Self-Reported Survey Results	Your Answer
1. In the past month, how often did you experience a breathing problem?	4 or more times a week (0 points)
2. In the past month, how often did your breathing wake you up?	2–3 times a week (5 points)
3. In the past month, how often did your breathing problem prevent you from participating in normal activities, such as walking or running?	One a week (10 points)
4. In the past 3 months, how often did you use an inhaler to treat a breathing problem?	2–3 times a week (5 points)
Total Score (Note a score less than 80 may mean your breathing problem is not well-managed)	45

Possible questions for this scenario include:

- ▶ What information is omitted from the survey that could be affecting the patient's asthma?
- ▶ What conclusion can you take away from the results of the survey?
- ▶ Based on this information, how would you decide whether to write the patient a stronger prescription or discuss the proper use of her current inhalers?

Tradeoffs or Risk Management

According to Clark (2012), tradeoffs or risk management scenarios assess how learners apply knowledge to make decisions or take actions when there may be multiple ways to handle the situation. These types of questions lend themselves wonderfully to leadership and soft skills topics. Here's an example scenario:

You are a director of a community service organization. The staff has noticed that some items have been missing from the office, including a laptop. There are concerns about how much access there is to the office area, and some of your direct reports suggest increasing security measures. Others have vocalized that they don't want to deal with a change like that. As the director, it is up to you to decide how best to prevent theft from occurring in the office.

Possible questions for this scenario include:

- ▶ How would you handle a situation if a direct report accused someone of stealing things from the office?
- ▶ What considerations would you need to know when determining your next steps for dealing with the situation?
- ▶ How would you address safety concerns with clients served by the community service organization?

Operations Decisions and Tasks

According to Clark (2012), a desired outcome of an operations decisions and tasks scenario is to be able to take actions in a simulated environment. These types of assessments are great for leadership development or applying new content to a task for the first time. Here's an example scenario:

You are a widget maker who is using a new machine with an internal camera. This is the control panel of the machine. To start your first operation to make a widget, you'll need to input the buttons in the correct order so you don't damage the widget material.

Possible questions for this scenario include:

▶ If the widget material is damaged, how do you annotate that in the system?

▶ From the control panel, how would you realign the camera?

Development and Design

According to Clark (2012), a desired outcome of a development and design scenario is to be able to create a work product that meets the scenario's parameters. These types of assessments can be applied to operations management and enhanced product knowledge. Here's an example scenario:

You are a website developer working with a large cat food manufacturer who is releasing plant-based cat food for vegan felines. The manufacturer wants to beat a competitor to market and wants a website landing page to create hype. The landing page needs to have information about where to purchase the cat food, nutrition facts, and videos or gifs of happy vegan feline taste testers. They also want to get a veterinarian endorsement but haven't shared that information with you. They have given little guidance on the preferred look and feel of the landing page aside from telling you they want it to be "purrfect."

Possible questions for this scenario include:

▶ What are some expectations you should consider setting with your client to help meet their goals and deadlines?

▶ What are some visualizations and structures you'd recommend for their website?

▶ What are some constraints you've identified in this project?

Planning or Resource Management

According to Clark (2012), a desired outcome of a planning or resource management scenario is to be able to align and coordinate dissemination of information among a group or across an enterprise. This type of assessment is great for enhancing decision making and leadership development. Here's an example scenario:

> You are a regional director in the Federal Emergency Management Agency (FEMA). The National Hurricane Center reports that Hurricane Bib is approximately 300 miles off the coast of your local shoreline. The local office of the National Hurricane Center issues a hurricane watch for large portions of the coast, including your community. Currently a Category 1 hurricane, Bib continues to gain strength and is projected to make landfall in 48 to 72 hours. Forecasts predict the storm will strengthen overnight, upgrading to a Category 3 hurricane.
>
> Possible questions for this scenario include:
> - ▶ What information is shared among the organization?
> - ▶ What information is shared with the general public?
> - ▶ What, if any, decisions should be made at this time?

Reflection: Going through each type of scenario learning domain, which one do you currently use most frequently? Which one are you going to try next?

Composition of Assessment

When you are creating assessments for your learning experiences, have you ever thought about the composition of the overall assessment? Do the questions you are asking align to the tasks and KPIs you want the learning experience to address? I recommend this conversation go beyond the subject matter experts to people who are doing the work. Explore different data sources to see if there are any performance checklists or other materials that can give you a clear picture of how people are assessed on the job. Having this additional information can help you better align your assessments.

Additionally, I became more versed with the types of assessment, specifically formative and summative. A way to remember the difference between them is that a *formative assessment* is "for learning," or it is a way to assess that your learners have a grasp of the content. A *summative assessment*, on the other hand, is "of learning," or it is an opportunity to apply the content. Both have their place but only if the assessments are written in a way that is aligned to the goals of the learning experience and what someone needs to do on the job. Remember, task analyses are a wealth of information when creating assessments, specifically the "How does a new person make a mistake?" and "How do they know they did it right?" columns.

Conclusion

Effective assessments take work to create but are critical to crafting a good learning experience. To check yourself during the product step, take inventory of how your assessments compare to your KPIs and what someone will do because of your learning experience.

30/60/90 Plan

Here is a 30/60/90 plan to get you started.

30 days: Explore your assessments via styles and analytics.

60 days: Create measurable assessments that measure content knowledge, not deduction skills.

90 days: Iterate and reflect on what has worked and what hasn't.

Chapter 8
The Red Pen

In this chapter, we will explore:

◉ Quality assurance criteria

◉ Types of feedback

Now that you have created the perfect learning experience, you are finished, right? Not so fast. It's critical that you share your learning experience for feedback. I like to have the learning and development team review it prior to sending it to stakeholders. I also like receiving different types of feedback. The pieces I look for during this stage are team peer feedback on the experience, stakeholder feedback on accuracy, and delivery review feedback. Let's go through each item in detail.

Team Peer Review

When building my team from scratch in a manufacturing role, I found that each team member had a different standard of what good learning design looked like. The same was true with feedback. When a team member would ask for feedback, some were more diligent and detail oriented than others. To help with this discrepancy, I created a quality assurance checklist. Let's review the criteria and their explanations.

Instructional Content

✓ **The content is accurate and signed off by a SME (designer only).** The stakeholder blessed the content before the learning experience was built and signed off on its accuracy.

✓ **The content references appropriate work instructions or standards.** The user knows about the corresponding technical documentation (if appliable) that supports the learning experience.

✓ **The content has an estimated time for completion.** The user can tell how long it will take to complete the learning experience and can appropriately plan when to complete it.

✓ **The content has appropriate instructions throughout to guide the user.** The user is given instructions on how to interact with and navigate through the learning experience.

✓ **The content is sequenced in a logical manner.** Every lesson and module of an online course should be logically sequenced. For every module or lesson, the introduction should be the first chapter. Similarly, all quizzes and tests should appear only after the relevant information has been taught. The content taught inside each lesson should be put in order, from basic information to complex ideas. While planning the sequence, keep yourself in the shoes of the user, and think as if they don't know anything about the subject.

Grammar and Typography

✓ **There are no missing titles.** Confirm all headers and titles are present. Titles should be big and bold and should be clearly identifiable as a header or title.

✓ **There is no missing or incorrect punctuation.** Not having punctuation in the right place can possibly change the meaning of a sentence. Make sure punctuation is placed correctly and consistently. Some of the common punctuation marks used are full stops or periods, commas, colons, semicolons, question marks, exclamation points, brackets, braces, apostrophes, hyphens, and quotation marks.

✓ **Text positioning and formatting is appropriate (including font choice, bolded text, and font size).** Consistently positioning text is important especially where there are visual elements or graphics involved. If there are multiple images on a slide and the text is spilled all over the place, this can confuse the user about which content is related to which visual, and wrong information can be perceived by the learner.

✓ **There are no spelling mistakes.** Double-check the spelling and correct use of every word.

✓ **There are no broken links.** Even though this is not a grammar check, links are a part of the text, so they are included in this section. Many times we add links to external sources for additional reading or references. Make sure these links work. Not just the external links, but there could also be internal links pointing to different modules or lessons, or links to downloadable content. Check that all links point to the right resources.

✓ **All acronyms are defined.** Define acronyms that learners may not know. For example, ADDIE—which stands for analysis, design, development, implementation, and evaluation. Now, you would have known that already, but imagine someone reading ADDIE for the first time and being clueless about what it means.

✓ **Words are appropriately cased.** The casing of words can simply be defined as using uppercase and lowercase letters appropriately.

✓ **All instructional content makes sense.** Does the content flow, and can a beginner follow it?

Audio, Video, Voice-Over, and Music

✓ **The quality of audio is superior, and audio is used appropriately.** Check that the sound is not muffled, or the playback is too fast or slow. Sometimes, the audio can be too high pitched or low pitched. In either case, it would not make a good learning experience. Moreover, every user might have different kinds of earphones or speakers, so it's necessary to have audio quality optimized for all kinds of devices.

✓ **The pronunciation of words is accurate in voice-overs.** All words should be pronounced correctly. Don't assume the voice-over artist (if used) did this correctly, so do a quality assurance check of every word.

✓ **The background music is tasteful and doesn't distract from interaction.** Be sure background music (if used) is necessary, the volume is soothing, and it helps the user focus. Try not to add popular music as a background sound because the user might spend time thinking about which song the music is from instead of focusing on the content.

✓ **The voice-over is complete and not missing any parts.** There can be scenarios when either the voice-over was missed or wasn't added to the correct part of the video or slide. Maybe it was muted, or the volume was lowered during editing. Check if there are any missing pieces of audio voice-over.

✓ **Videos are created in a way that helps users understand the content.** The video is engaging and keeps users' attention and brings life to the content.

✓ **Video graphics are of high quality.** All images in videos are of good quality and are easy to read and see.

✓ **Videos have captions for any speaking.** Video captions are timed appropriately and accurately.

✓ **Videos have progress bars for users to slow down and speed up the playback speed.** Incorporating this feature in a course is advisable because it allows the user to take the course at their own pace. Check if users can adjust the speed, then check if the default playback speed is set to normal so that anyone can easily understand and gain knowledge from the course.

✓ **Captions and audio can be toggled by users.** The user can adjust audio levels and toggle captions if desired.

Visual Design

✓ **The organization's logo is used in the experience for branding.** Per branding expectations, use the organization's logo in the learning experience.

✓ **Colors are appropriate and do not distract from the learning experience.** Every color represents a different emotion and is perceived in a certain way by the human brain. For example, try to visualize a "yes" check mark in red and an "x" reject mark in green. It is probably the opposite of what you are used to, right? Similarly, we have a certain expectation for most colors. Try to make sure the right colors are used.

✓ **Visual details such as graphs and charts can be clearly seen, and images can be zoomed in on and still be readable.** Let's consider an example of a project management related course. One lesson is about how to prepare project timelines. This lesson will have numbers and text mentioned in the graphics, but if the graphic is not high resolution, the user will be unable to figure out the content. All the user sees are blurry images with lines and unidentifiable symbols (which are supposed to be numbers and symbols). This check also applies when learners are being taught how to use a tool and the video or images are not clear. It would be difficult for a user to know what button to click and what information to look for, where to look for it, and how it should look. Therefore, use visuals that show every detail that you intend to show to the users.

✓ **Graphics are appropriate for the audience.** This might not be applicable in every instance, but you should check for any sensitive visual that could have a negative impact on learners. Also, avoid using any branded images without having proper permission, as visuals that are subject to copyright can attract legal issues.

✓ **White space is used tastefully throughout the learning experience.** Having too much white space can reduce the amount of information, but having very little white space can make it difficult for the user to focus.

✓ **The learning experience is responsive (mobile).** If you build in an auto-response tool, skip this.

✓ **Icons are clear and easy to read.** Icons are readable and it is easy to understand what they mean.

✓ **Text and images are in alignment.** Alignment makes a huge impact in the overall look and feel of any digital content. Text and icons should be formatted so that they look centered and in sync with one another. If they're not aligned well, learners may assume an A icon is displayed for a B point instead of an A, which can lead to confusion.

✓ **No text or images are cut off throughout the learning experience.** Check that no text or graphics are cut off from the screen. This can happen in slides, documents, downloadable content, transcripts, subtitles, and other visuals. It can also happen when the course content is not responsive to screen size, so some portion of content gets cut off when viewed on different screens. To fix this issue, you will have to do cross-browser testing.

Course Navigation (UI)

✓ **Navigation buttons are consistent throughout and function appropriately.** The navigation user interface is consistent throughout the course and points to the appropriate parts of the learning experience.

✓ **The user doesn't get stuck in certain interactions (for example, a blank screen or no buttons).** The learning experience flows, and there are no points where the user can't move forward or backward in the program.

✓ **Additional information that is accessed by hovering over text opens correctly.** If used, more information is provided by hovering over the interaction instructions.

Interactivity (UX)

✓ **Items that are clickable work for every lesson.** Buttons, images, and charts work.

✓ **Users get feedback in activities.** Any question or activity should provide more feedback to the user than "That's right" or "That's wrong."

✓ **Submit buttons work appropriately.** Submit buttons are used on forms, tests, and quizzes and should actually work when pressed.

✓ **Accordion menus work correctly.** Accordions collapse and reopen appropriately, and all tabs work.

✓ **Course progress is denoted.** The user can see their progress. (Rise automatically does this.)

✓ **Drop-downs work appropriately.** Any drop-downs (buttons or text boxes) open.

Assessment and Evaluation

✓ **The learning experience has formative and summative assessments.** The user goes through formative assessments (for learning and knowledge checks) as well as a summative assessment (of learning, to apply the content in a work-based scenario).

✓ **The learning experience has a work-based scenario.** The user is asked to to complete a work-based scenario to demonstrate how they can apply the content to their job and why they should care.

✓ **Assessments provide feedback.** Feedback is clear and provides information about why the answer is correct or incorrect.

✓ **The evaluation form is present and opens.** The evaluation form is open and can be used.

✓ **The evaluation form can be filled out completely and records responses.** The evaluation form functions appropriately and records responses.

✓ **The assessment is scored appropriately.** Let's say the learner attempted an assessment multiple times and had different scores every time. In this case, we can either show them their latest marks or all marks separated by attempt.

Technology

✓ **The learning experience has been tested in multiple browsers (for example, Microsoft Edge and Google Chrome).** When a course is opened on a desktop in the Google Chrome browser window, everything looks perfect, but when the same course is opened in a Microsoft Edge browser window, the visuals get cut off or some features do not function as intended. Test your content across browsers to ensure consistency.

✓ **Mouse clicks and keyboards function smoothly.** For a user to engage and interact with the course, it is essential that the course allows access to the mouse and keyboard of the user's computer system. Check if the mouse and keyboard inputs work wherever there is an action required from the user.

✓ **The LMS records data correctly.** A course must be uploaded in some system for the learner to be able to access it, like an LMS. Once the course is uploaded, run through it once in the LMS as a user to make sure everything functions as intended.

Accessibility and Inclusion

✓ **A wide variety of characters are used throughout the learning experience.** People in stock images are diverse in age, gender, race, and ability.

✓ **Inclusive language is used throughout the learning experience.** Language is respectful, gender neutral, and open throughout the content. For example, replace *manpower* with *labor*.

Reflection: Now that you've had an opportunity to look at my internal quality assurance criteria, what does yours look like? Do you do a separate team review and stakeholder review?

Stakeholder Review

Stakeholders, if you can get them to give you feedback, will have no problems telling you their opinions. I've had stakeholders get heated up over the shade of blue I used on a component and over the music I selected for a course. The quality assurance procedures put in place during a team review should also improve many of the design choices. Jonathan Couser (2021), an incredible learning and development leader, shared this pro-tip with me when I interviewed him for a podcast episode about ways to triage feedback. Couser suggested that when asking for feedback on learning experiences, set the expectations with the stakeholders using "Level 1" and "Level 2" feedback.

Level 1 feedback is the essential, workable feedback we are seeking from stakeholders and includes the following:

- **Accuracy.** Is the content accurate? Is there anything that could be deemed false depending on someone's role in the company?
- **Terminology.** Are the words correct? Are acronyms spelled out? Will anyone going through the learning experience have trouble understanding what the content is referring to?
- **Point of view (POV).** Is there any additional information learners will need to interact with the learning experience effectively? Is the content written from the perspective of someone who is doing the related task?
- **Grammar and spelling.** Are there any mistakes that we missed?

That's it. If they have additional feedback, classify it as Level 2 (or preferences). During my time in higher education, I came up with a steadfast rule for implementing feedback: If it doesn't have a pedagogical impact or affect the accuracy of the learning experience, I will consider it in future revisions and updates. This includes someone's favorite song, color, and clipart. I'm not kidding when I say I've had stakeholders insist on things like this throughout my career. Don't let them derail all of your hard work over something that will not enhance it.

It's not just about the content, however, it's about the experience. I think it's critical to assess a learning experience pre-launch from an accessibility lens. I went into more detail about building accessibility into design in chapter 6, but Figure 8-1 is an example of a checklist you may use during the red pen phase to assess how effectively you incorporated it.

Figure 8-1. Example of Level 2 Feedback: Accessibility Considerations (POUR)

☐ **Perceivable**
Learning experience has alternative text for images, captioning is available on videos or a transcript is provided, there is a sufficient contrast between text and background, no content relies on color alone, and text is readable and legible.

☐ **Operable**
Learning experience has clear structure with mark up and headings, links are descriptive, learning experience is tested for keyboard accessibility, sufficient time is provided for interaction and response, and content is avoided that can trigger seizures.

☐ **Understandable**
Learning experience has clear directions and models, and language is consistent and plain throughout the learning experience.

☐ **Robust**
Learning experience has gone through a full accessibility check, metadata is descriptive, and content is tested on a variety of platforms.

Delivery Review

You need to see the product in its intended form. I can't tell you how many mistakes I've made because I didn't do the last spot check and missed something that was wrong. For digital learning experiences, this review includes uploading the content into the system where people will be accessing it. I've worked with folks in my career who even came up with usability testing for these instances, which included answering assessments incorrectly, using different browsers, or trying to break the learning experience. This "bug squashing," as it was often called when I was at Amazon, was critical to making sure that the learning experience worked correctly in the system it would be housed in. If the learning experience is more tactile, like a piece of paper or a poster, print a test copy and evaluate its readability. Documents often look different on a screen than when printed, so don't trust the digital copy. Also, consider what someone has to do to access the content. Are there ways to streamline the process and make it easier for the user so they will want to return to it as needed?

Conclusion

To create a quality product, revisions need to happen. By having clear criteria in your quality assurance process and keeping the editing load as light as possible on stakeholders, you will set yourself and your team up for success.

30/60/90 Plan

To get started, use this 30/60/90 plan to help you on your journey.

30 days: Explore your quality assurance documents and standards.

60 days: Identify one to two quality assurance standards you'd like to start using in your own process.

90 days: Iterate and reflect on what has worked and what hasn't.

Chapter 9
The Message and the Takeoff

In this chapter, we will explore:

- The criticality of the learning experience's message
- Monitoring the release of the LXD product

Have you ever been haunted by the thought of an unexpected mandatory training? You know, the one that hits during a week of pure chaos when you already have so many other obligations? The one that you are struggling to figure out how to squeeze time in for? The one that you have no idea why you need it?

I'd venture to say that many of you have been in that position. After all the work that has gone into building the learning experience to this point, wouldn't it be horrible if you rolled something out and people didn't know what it was? Sadly, this happens too often, so it's critical that you not only craft the message to accompany the learning experience but also monitor the progress of the LXD product once it is made live.

The Message

Learning experiences fail when people don't understand why they need to do something. I've seen so many mistakes and frustrations come out of a lack of communication about new programs. If possible, I encourage pairing your learning experience with a communication campaign. Adults want to know the *why* behind something. Here are some of the key aspects for the message:

- **How will it be communicated?** While email may be your default response, I encourage you to think beyond that. How many emails do we all miss on a daily basis? When I used to work for Amazon, their system would often push out a SYSKA, or "stuff you should know about" message, as a banner at the top of the system some employees used. When I was in manufacturing, there was a system that not only pushed out messages but required employees to acknowledge them to continue. Of course, some just hit the button and continued on, but the system also allowed the message to be sent an additional way, such as a copy back to the user's email. Finally, don't assume that you should just tell the folks who will be attending the training, as it's critical that their leadership knows too. Even better if they have been informed ahead of time.
- **Overview: What is happening?** Don't underestimate the power of this portion either. When you are putting together the message, be clear about expectations. Is it an in-person instructor-led training event or an e-learning course? Is it something that needs to be done soon, or will they have some time (in 30 days or so)?
- **Purpose: Why are we doing it?** Providing additional context from your kickoff meeting and intake form can also be helpful.
- **What business priority does this affect?** How does this affect the full organization?
- **Roles and responsibilities: How does this affect you?** What is expected of the individual and how will it affect them?
- **Next steps:** What will they need to do to enroll (if anything)? Is there any prework and will there be reminders?

In the past I've used a communications template with these questions on it that I filled in during this step. This step can sneak up on you, so it's good to have these questions ready to go at a moment's notice. Depending on your organization, you may need to get approvals and permission from HR, legal, communications, IT, or other functions to send the message. I found this out the hard way while working at Amazon when I put together a message to share about a course being put on people's transcripts. The list of email addresses for the target audience was wrong, so I sent the message to the wrong batch of folks.

So many tools, from learning management systems to productivity apps, allow these communications to go out to people; however, I'd caution you to be consistent in the medium you use. For example, don't send an email for one program and use Slack for another. Also, get feedback if possible from other departments, such as IT and HR, for guidance on company policies and procedures for sending mass messages.

The message is also an opportunity to flex your creative muscles— consider building a teaser trailer or use it to launch a campaign around the product. Don't assume people know anything about your program. This is an opportunity to explain why the learning experience was needed and how it will help participants in their jobs. Once the message is crafted and sent out, then you are ready for the takeoff.

Reflection: How do you share the message of your LXD products?

The Takeoff

Once we launch a product—the takeoff—we usually have some anxiety. After you roll out a learning experience, you should observe the takeoff and consider how the program is influencing the learners. If it's a live session, attend the first one. Go on a gemba walk, which is when you walk the floor and ask for feedback. If you don't have that opportunity, set up a focus group to gather feedback.

Please don't think I'm downplaying the pride you will feel once something launches; I get giddy too. One of my favorite stories from a friend of mine, e-learning developer Joseph Suarez, was about the pride he felt after launching one of his first e-learning courses. Joe put in a lot of work to build it and wanted to walk around the organization to get feedback. While he was walking around, he found someone asleep in front of their computer with his e-learning program on the screen. Talk about a wake-up call! I love this story so much because I'm sure we've all had learning experiences do the same thing. This story also ended up being my inspiration for diving into learner engagement and became a joke in a presentation I did about learner engagement.

Once you launch a learning experience, the project is not over, even though this is when many people stop in their process. It's not enough to give someone a content sandwich. You need to be proactive in your approach to ensure that you deliver what people need to influence the metric you agreed on during the kickoff. By closely monitoring data during the takeoff and planning to continue the conversation, you can do that. Content isn't enough alone, and it takes a cross-functional partnership to affect results.

When I worked in a call center, one of the things many associates looked forward to was logging out of production (the call center work queue) to work on other activities. One lesson I'm thankful I learned early on was about the impact of others in the work that we did. Whenever we created a training product, we worked with our workflow partners to schedule time for associates to be able to either go to a training session or do it individually on their computers. By planning for the event, staffing numbers could be changed or other sites could take a larger queue of customer contacts during this time to balance out the lower active associate head count in the queue. Too many training products are tossed onto the workload of folks who have plenty to do but often don't have the luxury of a workflow analysis team to give them the time out of their day-to-day activities.

But time is only one part of the equation here. If we don't take the time to provide support and follow-up, we are essentially setting up our LXD products to fail because we can't effectively measure how they did. Our role in preparing and delivering the product is just the first step; we should also be proactive in our messaging along with monitoring during the takeoff. Did you learn how to ride a bicycle or drive a car? It was likely a scary experience as you were trying something new. But the more you do something, the more comfortable you become. Think of your LXD products as an opportunity to prepare people to excel and apply the content. Ultimately it is selfish to think that only a learning experience will "solve" the problem.

Conclusion

The message and takeoff are two critical steps that can help you communicate the value of the learning experience to the audience and continue to help support them as they are using it.

30/60/90 Plan

Use this 30/60/90 day plan to get started:

30 days: Explore your own communication and monitoring processes.

60 days: Identify one to two aspects you'd like to work on and gather resources.

90 days: Iterate and reflect on what has worked and what hasn't.

Chapter 10
The Results

In this chapter, we will explore:

- ◉ Creating better evaluation questions
- ◉ Leveraging evaluation data
- ◉ Continuing the conversation

In chapter 7, we talked about assessment—how to measure the user's acquisition of knowledge and skills. Now, it's time to talk about evaluation—how to measure the overall learning product's effectiveness at every level, from user reaction through organizational results.

Too often, I see evaluations not being used in learning experiences, and when they are, they gather superficial data. I remember attending a conference where I met someone who said they had a 100 percent success rate with their learning experiences. I was skeptical. After they provided no clarifying information, I asked how they rated success. They told me that they earn 10s on their evaluations. Their evaluation metric was a net promoter score, which tallies answers to the question, "On a scale of 0–10, how likely are you to recommend this to a co-worker or friend?" This metric doesn't measure actual application of the training on the job. If someone creates courses for the sake of selling them to other organizations or is an off-the-shelf vendor, there may be some value to the net promoter score as a metric of how well their courses could sell, but for those embedded in organizations who have to demonstrate long-term performance improvement due to training, I'd argue its value is small as it gives no indication of the confidence or application of the material to the work.

An evaluation model that is used often is the Kirkpatrick Model of Evaluation. In 2010, the model was updated to the Kirkpatrick New World Evaluation Model to provide more guidance on Levels 3 and 4 based on user feedback.

The four levels, in short, are:

- **Level 1: Reaction.** This is typically the "smile sheet" given at the end of training sessions asking users to rate how they liked the experience.
- **Level 2: Learning.** This roughly correlates to what we discussed in chapter 7, assessment: How well did learners acquire skills or knowledge?
- **Level 3: Behavior.** This takes the previous level a step further: Are learners using the skills and knowledge they acquired back on the job?
- **Level 4: Results.** This is frequently described as the hardest level to measure: How have the changed behaviors affected the organization's overall performance?

Kirkpatrick is an evaluation classic because the four levels (reaction, learning, behavior, and results) are clear and logical when evaluating the impact of training. It's been my experience, however, that many learning experience designers aren't even measuring Level 1 appropriately. Let's look at how each level can be measured to gain the most valuable insights available.

Level 1

Level 1 feedback, or reaction, measures participant satisfaction. While this seems simple (asking users how they felt about the training course), ask yourself if you're asking these questions appropriately. Often, questions are focused on what I call "creature comforts," such as whether learners liked the training session. We won't win any popularity contests just because our users state they like what we made. Instead, ask a question that measures whether learners thought they would be able to use what they learned on the job. By giving users a way to share information about the relevance of the content, we're able to gain actionable data. If we receive feedback that it isn't relevant, that is a problem, so we should remember to phrase our questions to elicit helpful feedback.

Here's another Level 1 tip: Depending on the organization and the technologies available, I like using forms that are tied to people's accounts in the organization. In other words, you know who they are when they fill out your evaluation, and the information is tied to the authentication of the user in other systems. By collecting this data first, you help save participants' time instead of asking them to fill out their names and email addresses. Having this information also gives you a way to follow-up with that person. When I was working in manufacturing, we set up our evaluations in Microsoft Forms, and just by tying it to the learner's account automatically, we increased our response rate. Also, don't worry about doing anything nefarious; if this feature is active, there will be a note at the top of the form that indicates the form is collecting their email address.

Level 2

Level 2 feedback, or learning, can be evaluated in several ways; although, much like Level 1, it's easy to miss the mark. Level 2 focuses on skills and attitudes and is often evaluated by summative assessments. My cautionary tale reveals that many assessments are poorly written and don't measure much beyond deduction skills. If you can create rigorous assessments, including multiple-choice questions and work-based scenarios, you will receive better data in Level 2. To measure for Level 2 feedback, try doing pre- and post-assessments, specifically asking people their level of proficiency before and after the training course.

When I transitioned to leading a learning and development department in a corporate setting, I had more autonomy to steer the evaluation ship. While the organization was not mature in the learning and development function, I found that it wasn't too hard to implement evaluation into my team's work. My North Star for guiding evaluation was Will Thalheimer's book, *Performance Focused Learner Surveys*. I wish I had read it sooner in my career, as it made a lasting impact on me. In his book, Thalheimer posed a question that I immediately knew would be a cornerstone of my evaluation strategy going forward, which I'll paraphrase: *After you've com-pleted the learning experience, how confident are you in applying this content to your job?* Instead of offering participants an open-ended response option, Thalheimer recommends using a modified Likert scale of pre-selected choices ranging from "I have significant blind spots and need additional support" (similar to level 1 of a Likert scale, low confidence) up to "I have expert level confidence, and I can teach a peer" (similar to level 5 of a Likert scale, extremely high confidence). This question is so powerful because it allows for appropriate follow-up actions to support people as they apply the content to their jobs.

Level 3

Level 3 feedback, or behavior, according to Kirkpatrick and Kirkpatrick (2016), is the most important because training alone won't deliver cross-enterprise performance improvement. Level 3 explores behavior on the job, and while we often aren't the frontline managers of the people in our organizations, this is when the need for partnerships and relational equity are key. Leaders are busy, so consider ways you can ask them for information about how people are performing better on the job. I've been able to get in front of leaders by asking for time in operations calls or other meetings leaders attend. I try not to take more than five minutes to tell them I'm looking for feedback on how their employees are performing the task they received training on, and I'm interested in any specific examples they want to share. I also bring a form I've created for them to add their examples to so I can follow up. Many times, this data highlights the need for performance support—such as quick videos, gifs, or job aids—to help users perform the tasks better. Targeted follow-up is a nice way to continue supporting people, even after the formal learning experience has ended.

One frequently missing piece of evaluation is the coaching element of a great learning experience. You know how you get better? You prac-tice. While learning experiences can offer practice opportunities, there will need to be additional coaching on the job to help people as they refine their skill development. Following up with users after the learning experience and asking a callback question about their progress can help determine the need for additional coaching. Remember, all great learning experiences are partnerships and collaborations, so with this information, you can advocate for more resources or go directly to managers and supervisors to see what you can do to continue your support. Remember, we are in the people business and should be available for this additional support and iteration.

Level 4

Level 4 feedback, or results, is the most difficult to measure. If you follow the process outlined in this book and you seek alignment on specific KPIs and tasks, results should be easier to meet. Too often, there is no clear criteria to appropriately measure Kirkpatrick Level 4. With the support of data from across your organization, you should be set on numbers. Please note that it is frequently difficult to make the case that training alone influenced the numbers. Thus, it's critical to do a full analysis before developing a learning experience to help control for environmental factors and other things that can affect the data.

So, what and how do we evaluate for impact? To start, it's important to build bridges for people to be champions of your learning experiences. What does this mean? Engage with people who use your learning experiences. Don't rely on only subject matter experts and project stakeholders. Talk to people who do the work. If you can't visit them in person, see what you can do to engage with them virtually. If that's not an option, consider what type of feedback systems you can modify or create to get feedback from those people, such as a Slack channel, a dedicated email address, or an embedded form. The bottom line is if you aren't directly engaging with the people on the other end, what exactly are you doing?

Following Up

Evaluation, however, isn't the end of the road. Remember that while learning experience design is the content and the context, a missing piece is the environment. No matter our best efforts, training does not fix a lack of accountability. But I don't mean accountability in a punitive sense. Let me give you an example.

There is a new process adopted at an organization for procurement. Everyone is expected to use the new process by the beginning of the second quarter with the old process sunsetting at that time. Everyone has been trained on the new process, and additional performance support has been implemented including a digital adoption platform (DAP) and job aids to support common processes. The second quarter begins, and most departments transition smoothly; however, one department and its leadership refuse to change and are still using the old system—pushing through requests as exceptions.

Your evaluation methodology is flawed if you do not take into account the political and environmental factors for success. While you are often not in the position to enforce compliance, you are in the position however to follow up on the implementation by asking questions about how it is going and touching base with your stakeholders. Those stakeholders then have to decide how they will handle compliance. I've been perplexed several times by stakeholders who have no context and assume everything is going perfectly. By following up, you can transition the position of your department from a transactional partner to become a consultative business partner.

Furthermore, after the content is delivered, you should also consider how it can be reinforced and supported. One way to provide meaningful support is by touching base with various frontline and middle managers to understand how they engage with their direct reports. If they have regular group meetings, consider asking them if you can take a few minutes to present a report or provide additional context via talking points. These talking points can be given directly to frontline and middle managers and can help spark conversations and provide additional context they may need to apply the content to their jobs. By being a part of these departmental meetings, you'll not only build your organizational relational equity, but also have an opportunity for some voice of the customer work. After all, we are in the people business, and we would not have jobs if it weren't for the folks we support in our organizations.

Conclusion

Evaluation is a continuous process at every level of the organization your learning experience touches. As you practice, you'll learn how to adapt each element to the needs and desired results of your learners. Next up, I will delve into what LXD looks like in different settings based on my professional experience.

30/60/90 Plan

Looking to apply some evaluation nuggets from this chapter to your content? I encourage you to use this 30/60/90 plan as a starting point and create your own plan because evaluation can look different from organization to organization.

30 days: Audit your current evaluation strategy and select a question or method to try.

60 days: Incorporate the aspect in your evaluation process and ask for feedback from users and team members.

90 days: Iterate and reflect on what has worked and what hasn't.

Chapter 11
Where We Do the Work

In this chapter, we will explore the settings where LXD takes place, including:

- Higher education
- Corporations
- Consulting

I've had the pleasure of working as a practitioner in higher education, in corporate organizations, and as a consultant throughout my career. I've enjoyed aspects of each setting—they are certainly unique and bring multiple challenges to creating a meaningful learning experience. My experiences have varied; to highlight these nuances, I want to explore what LXD looks like in each. This is a way for you to learn about a setting you may not have had the opportunity to work in and to grow your own perspectives of learning experience design. Because much of the content is influenced by my own experiences, however, please note that some of the considerations may not always be factors; your mileage may vary.

Reflection: In a few words, describe the setting you work in. As you read about different settings, what overlap do you see and what is unique to yours?

Higher Education

Higher education can be a challenging environment for a learning experience designer. It can also be a nourishing environment, but that depends on many factors. Learning experience design can be done in two main ways in higher education: internal facing for staff and faculty and academic facing for students (who are paying tuition with the option of being in an enterprise online learning department or via individual colleges).

To apply for LXD roles in higher education, you need a formal advanced degree (a master's degree or a doctorate). When I conducted job description research in 2020, using Fisher's exact test, the results showed that there is a significant association ($p<0.001$) between the job setting and the educational requirement stated in the job description (North et al. 2021). In other words, in the higher education setting, more jobs required master's degrees or higher, and fewer jobs required only bachelor's degrees. This can be a barrier to entry for some professionals wanting to transition into a higher education instructional design role, but it's also something you can take advantage of, which I will mention more about in a moment.

Returning to the two ways LXD functions in higher education, being a learning experience designer internally for staff and faculty of the institution, much like in a corporate learning environment, will mean providing some type of learning experience to the employees of the university. Some of the topics can be about research compliance, campus safety, or onboarding for new employees (including student workers). You could be working in a college directly in this role or in an enterprise system like a collective human resource system.

Another setting within higher education is academic facing—creating learning experiences for students. Depending on how the institution is structured, this can be done via a consolidated service center such as a department of online learning for the entire university. There are many advantages of a consolidated service center creating student-facing learning experiences, including resources and accreditation. It's been my experience that these consolidated service centers are well funded and often do the work of accreditation, which ensures online courses can be recognized for college credit in the state or country the student lives in.

Learning experience design can also be done in specific colleges; for example, a learning experience designer may work in the College of

Medicine or the College of Social Work. Typically, these teams are smaller than a consolidated service center and only work on learning experiences in the field of the college.

In my personal experience as a college learning experience designer, my role was in the information technology (IT) part of the institution, and my broader team included IT help desk associates, developers, and marketing and communications professionals. Work requests were tracked via a ticketing system so even a quick email or instant message from faculty became a ticket.

Learning Experience Design in Action

In 2019, I worked as a senior instructional designer in the College of Education and Human Ecology at my institution. I was approached by a faculty member who was building out a new program in applied behavioral analysis (ABA). The program would be composed of multiple courses to prepare students to work with people on the autism spectrum. The faculty member was an ABA practitioner and was excited yet nervous about building courses online; specifically, she asked how students could apply the content to the future work they would be doing.

Based on the various program outcomes, which were predetermined by the university and needed to be upheld for accreditation, we worked together to identify what students would need to do in the classroom environment to be successful working with folks on the autism spectrum. This took a while because it was different than what the faculty member was used to, which was focusing on the cognitive piece of the content provided to students. I encouraged her to trust the process, and we started to work together on the first course, an introductory course.

The faculty member was the subject matter expert, and I was the instructional designer and developer. Throughout the building of the course, we worked in sync. I encouraged the faculty member to bring in her experience from the field, as these anecdotes would be rich examples for students to apply content to the real world. Much of this experience helped us build meaningful scenarios, provided students with the performance support they would need to lead their own classrooms, and, most of all, gave them ways to reflect throughout the process. I also added feedback mechanisms in the course that we'd use to make changes in real time, as needed, to adjust our approach to what the students needed to be successful. At the end of the course, the students not only complimented the content but also the emotional connections that helped them start to understand more about the barriers and possible solutions to the environmental, social, and other challenges someone on the autism spectrum would be up against.

The learning experience design process in this example was slightly modified from the process outlined in chapter 2 because in higher education, accreditation and learning objectives are often more important than key performance indicators. This doesn't mean KPIs (or being able to relate the content to performance) weren't important; in fact, being able to highlight the real-world applications in this course made it special to the students who were taking it. This also became a common thread for the other courses we developed and something that the students came to expect—they often said they would refer to previous course material for certain situations. None of this could have happened, however, without the faculty member's trust in me and my abilities. I'll discuss more about why this trust is important in an upcoming section about obstacles in this environment.

Benefits of Working in Higher Education

A highlight of working in higher education as a learning experience designer was the amount of time stakeholders, and even participants (staff and faculty), spent questioning my expertise. On the surface, this may sound negative, but I enjoyed the stimulating discussions. People who work at universities often have a vigorous curiosity for learning, so I'd get asked all kinds of questions from why I designed something a certain way to how to best facilitate a Zoom call or improve delivery methods in an in-person course. I found that when I leaned into my experience, they'd want more, wondering what theory or literature supported my reasoning. This challenged me to be on my game. For example, I packed the ABA courses with references to support what I created in the curriculum. I discovered faculty loved diving into the citations, using them to challenge their own perspectives and leaning into the experience I brought to the role. It also gave me an opportunity for the same reflection, which was something I came to love about my job. I was encouraged to read literature, research, and participate. This made me a better practitioner and, upon reflection, is something I'm grateful for.

To expand on the encouragement and need to continue learning and researching, my favorite benefit of working in higher education was the educational support. Because I was a staff member, 100 percent of my tuition was paid for. Not reimbursed, but paid on my behalf. I had moved to the area and was interviewing to find my next role when the higher education institution told me they offered free tuition to full-time staff, and that convinced me to take the job. Working in an environment that made attending classes easy was something I think I took for granted. I was not discouraged from taking classes in the middle of the day or leaving early to work on school assignments. Additionally, during my time in higher education, I started attending and speaking at conferences. I was encouraged to submit speaking proposals, and I often got most of my travel expenses covered by the institution if I was able to secure a speaking slot to waive my registration fee. I was even eligible for additional funding as a student. One time, this support was also extended to me to present my research at an international conference, and the opportunity to travel to a new country is something I'm glad I was able to do.

Obstacles of Working in Higher Education

Now, here is where it gets tricky—at many institutions, faculty own the intellectual property of their courses. In my experience, this can mean one of two things: Faculty are willing to partner with the learning experience designer, or faculty don't want anything to do with you. The latter is the worst-case scenario, and there were times when I was in this situation. Some faculty worry about you taking their content. When I worked with someone who felt like this, I tried to explain that while they were the subject matter experts, I was the process expert, and I truly wanted to support the students in their courses to have the best experience possible. Sometimes this worked, but other times it didn't. This was such a weird phenomenon for me, especially coming from the corporate sector where I signed stringent non-disclosure agreements (NDAs).

A common pain point for higher education learning experience designers is when faculty treat our expertise as technical support. I'd find myself thinking, "Sure, it's no problem to show you how to use Zoom again, but do you think your students will watch a one-hour lecture of you talking about the history of education?" Despite my best efforts to guide faculty in the direction of creating student-centered learning experiences, most of the time I was brushed off and reminded that I, as a staff member, didn't own their work.

Prior to working in higher education, I had worked at both Amazon and an adult education center where I had the autonomy to build learning experiences in ways that would appeal to the audience. When faculty didn't want to have anything to do with me, I found myself compromising my standards for learning experiences because my expertise was not supported in the system of the organization. In fact, I recall, for a specific project, being advised that I should lower my standards. We did use a quality assurance rubric called Quality Matters, but the only time that learning experiences were evaluated with Quality Matters was when faculty members decided to work with my group. In other words, it was not mandatory for faculty to work with me to build their courses. Those who did seek my help were either looking for guidance or were "voluntold," reluctantly, to reach out for help. The footprint of the courses I was able to assist was small because this population was relatively small. So students were mostly at the mercy of what their professor had the capability to create.

Ways to Incorporate LXD in Higher Education

If you can have a direct role in creating learning experiences in higher education, it can be rewarding yet challenging for many reasons. There are ways to encourage better practices when developing courses. From bringing in research to fighting for the students in academic-facing courses, you need to feel empowered to bring your expertise to the table. You can help make better learning experiences, and I've outlined some techniques to try in Table 11-1.

Table 11-1. Ways to Incorporate Learning Experience Design in Higher Education

Technique	Application
Use research to support your rationale for change.	Cite sources and provide journal articles and book recommendations. Many faculty members will appreciate this.
Continue to stress partnerships.	Encourage faculty members to become comfortable working with you; let them know their intellectual property is safe and you are trying to enhance their content by helping them deliver it clearly and concisely in a way that supports their students in reaching the learning outcomes.
Consider a portfolio of work.	Don't assume the faculty knows the breadth of what you can do. If you use technology, be sure to explain that it isn't one-size-fits-all and that it may or may not work for what they are looking to do. Also, if you can explain the rationale behind your design choices, backed up by research and citations, it will strengthen your profile.
Solicit testimonials.	When something you've created worked well, ask the faculty member for a testimonial. These can help build credibility for your work and get the word out that you can help others.

Corporate Settings

My time in higher education was a few years after I got my start in learning development and learning leadership when I worked in corporate settings. Like many folks, I am an "accidental instructional designer," which means, according to Cammy Bean (2023), someone who finds learning and development through the organization they work in via an alternative role. I started working for a call center in Huntington, West Virginia, as a communicator. After being there for a few months, I was promoted into a quality assurance analyst role. A small part of the job included training new hires on quality assurance procedures like following the telemarketing script and dealing with objections. Since there was a new-hire class every week, training became a task I did frequently. After my first training session, I absolutely fell in love with it and told my parents it's what I wanted to do. Later, I left the call center to work for Amazon. During my time there, I did a little bit of everything, but it was during my time spent working as an instructional designer that I knew I'd found something I wanted to do. Working for Amazon, and then at a workforce development center teaching adults business and life skills, I was fulfilled and learning a lot myself. Going to work didn't feel like a job; I genuinely loved what I did because I was able to see how my work helped people, especially at the workforce development center. When I left higher education in 2020, I moved into a corporate learning leadership role and set the foundation for a learning and development department in a manufacturing company. Eventually, I transitioned into a director role at a healthcare technology startup before going into consulting full time.

Like in higher education, there are many types of work done in corporate settings. A question I like to ask when interviewing for a job is where learning and development sits in the organization. I've had experience sitting in operations, IT, and HR. I've also heard through peers that learning and development can sit in an enterprise L&D department, on a sales enablement team, or in a customer success group. I prefer to work in roles in operations because I've found them to be the most influential, with more opportunities to experiment and be creative. This doesn't mean that all jobs in other corporate settings are this way; it is just my preference. Also, I think it is easier in operations to get feedback and access to the people you are designing for.

Learning Experience Design in Action

In 2021, the manufacturing company I worked for was growing rapidly, but we had a problem: The talent pipeline dried up due in part to the Great Resignation. The type of work most of the positions we were hiring for required machining experience; however, my organization approached machining a bit differently due to the type of material we created. My boss challenged me to come up with a way to take folks with limited experience and set them up for success as machinists. I was also able to add two machinists to the training team I managed. For both, it was their first formal training job, but the way they took to it was a proud moment for me; it will likely be in my retirement speech someday.

Enough with the warm fuzzy feelings. The three of us discussed what it meant to be a machinist, and it wasn't as simple as I had hoped. Narrowing down the machinist role ended up being complicated because the steps and processes could look different depending on the machine and the part of the manufacturing floor someone worked on. I asked if there was any agreement on the steps that someone performs to run a machine that we could use as a starting point. Building on what I mentioned in chapter 4 about task analyses, I asked about how to determine if people performed the steps correctly, what they need to perform the steps, and (my favorite) how people could make mistakes during each step.

Once we agreed on what the steps were, we continued our analysis by going onto the manufacturing floor and comparing what we saw to the steps we were looking for. Then came the ultimate challenge: How could we create an environment where folks could practice tasks critical to being a machinist in our learning experience without using the actual machines? My team got creative and worked with other stakeholders to develop activities such as assembling tools. They went above and beyond, creating both simulations of machines and a fake machine component, complete with air lines and foot pedals, to practice a critical step of loading a part in a machine that could make or break an operation.

The result of this work was a week-long performance-focused learning experience, targeted for new machinists on their second week on the job. The curriculum was mapped and scaffolded around daily themes, with content in the mornings such as machinist mathematics for calculations, overviews of machines and functions, and preventative maintenance. The afternoon sessions gave people an opportunity to practice tasks critical to their roles and allowed them to not only build confidence, but mastery. If anyone made a mistake, one of the expert instructors would walk back through the steps with them to see what they did and help them understand where they'd gone wrong. Let me be clear: We wanted them to make mistakes. This wasn't difficult thanks to the sensitivity of tools used to measure the material, the techniques for handling the material, and the delicate components needed to make everything work. If something broke, we replaced it and moved on. At the end of the week, the students took a performance test going through every step to run the machine, which the instructor observed and evaluated using a performance sheet. Students were also evaluated on using appropriate personal protective equipment (PPE), cleaning up each station appropriately (because the material could be damaged easily in a dirty station), and putting their tools back in the appropriate spaces. This type of additional evaluation was based on the 5S system—sort, set in order, shine, standardize, and sustain. (5S is a lean principle used in manufacturing, which they learned about in their first week of orientation. This exercise allowed them to apply the content from their first week.)

The LXD process I outlined in chapter 2 was primarily used to develop this learning experience. I was under such a tight deadline, however, that I paused the entire operations training team to work on it. This collaborative effort is one that I'm extremely proud of because it helped solve a real business problem, and our rapid growth as an organization depended on it. The talent of everyone on the team was needed to pull it off.

To briefly share the scope of the project, during the span of two to three months, we collectively created more than 12 Articulate Storyline interactions (such as machine simulations), more than 10 video clips highlighting machine processing, more than 15 PowerPoint slide presentations (used during the in-person lab portion), one amazing SharePoint platform (with everything laid out by curriculum and open to everyone in the company to use as performance support), a full curriculum map, performance evaluation checklists, facilitator and participant guides, and hands-on labs. My team really outdid themselves, creating a tool-building station with custom tool holders, a stack of supplies, signs, and decorations from the training room to describe each station. It brings a tear to my eye thinking about it now because it was such a collaborative effort and by far the best learning experience I've had the pleasure of working on. We put together 40 hours of curriculum, with at least 20 of those hours being hands-on practice and simulations. Did I mention that this week-long experience was also led by two brand-new to L&D facilitators? They did a fantastic job, and watching them grow their confidence and facilitation skills was a pleasure to witness.

Benefits of Working in a Corporation

While there are many benefits of working in a corporate environment, I think one of my favorites is the variety of work. In higher education, the variety I experienced was mostly due to me changing departments every year or two because I craved change and felt it was the only way to continue moving up in my career. Sometimes, I think corporate learning and development is like the tagline from the TV show *Pawn Stars*: "You'll never know what will come through that door." Variation is something I crave and need to be happy in a role. One day can be spent working on a request for training on software, and the next day I could be training on how to write a polite email.

Another benefit of working for a corporation is the space L&D occupies. While we aren't usually in the C-suite, we often aren't on the frontline of the organization either. This allows us to come to the table with neutral stances on issues. Perhaps it's my undergraduate education in journalism, but this neutrality appeals to me. If we don't ask the questions, who will? Who will ask, "Why"? Who will ask about the success metrics? It's not that our peers are negligent or have ill intentions, but most of the time they are too close to the project to see the forest for the trees.

Obstacles of Working in a Corporation

Like higher education, one obstacle in corporate settings occurs because people often come to you with an idea of what they want, and it can be hard to change their mind. Most stakeholders remember what it was like being a student in K–12 education or in college and assume that simply giving content to someone will train them. When I worked in leadership, I advocated on behalf of the team, but it was not always easy to handle. Sometimes, you have difficult stakeholders that will not budge. You must learn to pick your battles, as painful as it is, and start to chip away at their expectations to make the overall learning experience better for your audience.

Another obstacle in corporate settings is the speed at which stakeholders want our services. I can't tell you how many times in my career someone has reached out for training support on a Friday afternoon for a Monday training session or wanted me to magically make a video or e-learning course in half a day. This is challenging to deal with as an individual contributor, and you frequently need the support of your leadership because I've found many people don't like being told "no." Compounding this challenge is the fact that some organizations are not open to giving learning and development departments the autonomy to determine the best way to create a learning experience. So many organizations use lack of training as a scapegoat for all kinds of problems, but one thing training can never fix is an issue with accountability. I worked in an organization like this once, and I couldn't make the impact I wanted because of the larger issue with management incompetence and a fear of holding people accountable. Know what I did? I walked away. I'm grateful I was empowered enough and had options so I could leave, but I also know that depending on your level in an organization and in your career, this can be a tough decision. Ultimately, we exist to help our organizations help people be more productive, keep them safe, increase profits, and decrease costs. People don't work for organizations just to take training courses; they want to do their jobs!

Ways to Incorporate LXD in a Corporation

Regardless of where you sit in a corporation, there are many ways you can incorporate learning experience design in corporate settings. Know that nothing changes overnight, even if it feels like your organization moves at a rapid pace. Consider what alignment you can get before beginning your design, embrace the power of the people you serve in your learning experiences, and be patient with yourself in the process. Table 11-2 presents some strategies to try at your organization.

Table 11-2. Ways to Incorporate Learning Experience Design in a Corporation

Technique	Application
Align to a metric or KPI.	Use this alignment to help tailor what content needs to be included, what content you can exclude, and how you can further support your learners.
Show off your wins.	If you created an influential learning experience, mapped to a KPI, and provided value, show it off. If possible, see if you can get on the agenda for an all-hands meeting. Showing the value, not just telling stakeholders, of crafting a meaningful learning experience can help your business case transform to learning experience design.
Create an intake process.	Procurement has a process. IT has ticketing systems. Consider creating an intake process for requests that come to the L&D team. This can be challenging, so be sure to get buy-in from your leadership and convince them you want to plan and allocate resources appropriately. If a requester can't be bothered to give you information about the potential project, that should tell you what type of stakeholder they will likely be on the project.
Lean into HR for engagement surveys and process improvement groups with gemba walks.	Consider what your voice of the customer (VOC) efforts look like. See if you can access employee engagement surveys, participate in gemba walks, or create your own way to get time with people you serve. It matters so that you can get a pulse on emotional triggers to understand their environments more and potentially gain champions for new L&D projects.

Consulting

From large L&D consulting firms to independent consultants, there are many opportunities to work as an LXD consultant. Depending on the type of contract you are offered, you may be responsible for a full project or certain elements of a learning experience. Especially in the last few years, opportunities for project work—when you are expected to work for an organization for three to six months or more in a full-time capacity—have been popping up. Organizations hire consultants for a variety of reasons including to meet rapid project demands in their L&D departments. Another reason consultants may be hired is to clean up a big mess—the company may need someone to come in and fix issues. The work is often deliverables based on requirements that vary from the software you use to the way you keep the organization updated.

I've consulted on the side since 2017 and started mainly as a growth opportunity. I wanted to take on stretch assignments and found opportunities through freelancers, who needed certain parts of a project done and either lacked the bandwidth or didn't want to tackle them. Through my consulting work, I gained valuable skills in business communication and sales, and I picked up tricks along the way from others about L&D. This look "under the hood" across many industries helped inform my actions and ultimately made me a better practitioner. Also, when I left my role as director of L&D in 2022, this part-time consulting experience gave me the confidence to go out on my own full time.

Learning Experience Design in Action

I want to share a failure with you. In 2020, many higher education institutions needed help moving courses online. Many of them didn't create what I'd consider an online course but rather "emergency remote teaching" opportunities (Hodges et al. 2020). I took this idea a step further and considered it a *panicgogy*, or a spin-off of pedagogy but with more panic and less care for students and learning science.

I had an opportunity to consult with a university that was building online courses for the fall 2020 semester. My first impression was a good one; I was working directly with faculty in a college with oversight by the university's Enterprise Online Learning Division. They had strict project management deliverables. But this is where I made my first mistake— the payment would be rendered only after the course was delivered. No exceptions. Now, this isn't always bad, and I didn't think I'd have any issues because there was such an ordered front-end organization from the Enterprise Online Learning Division.

The course was about a business topic, and I scheduled a meeting with the faculty member. While he was accomplished and nice, it was clear from our first meeting that he would require a lot of hand-holding —not only helping him prepare the curriculum for online delivery but also encouraging him to move the course online. The faculty member did not hold back his thoughts—it was not a positive reaction. I tried my best to stay positive and provided a list of dates when I'd need things from him and scheduled a weekly check-in call. He told me I should come to his office to have these meetings. (At this point, I don't think he knew I was a contractor and not local.) I told him my location, and he couldn't believe I was working with him almost 1,500 miles away.

To make a long story short, it didn't work out. The faculty member, while nice, was resistant to moving the course online. The Enterprise Online Learning Department had such tight project deliverable deadlines that when I escalated our problems, they acted like I must be doing something wrong. I did get some content from the faculty member, but it was full of jargon and unusable visuals. In this case, I fired the client and walked away, receiving no payment for my time thanks to the contract provision of paying only for the final project. In this instance, I learned a valuable lesson too about the price and value of my time.

Benefits of Working as a Consultant

A primary benefit of being a consultant is that you are hired to conduct a task and for your expertise. I've found that when I serve as an internal practitioner as an employee of an organization, it can be more difficult to get buy-in and have people listen to me than when I work as a consultant. As a consultant, my expertise is often respected. Of course, that isn't always the case, but by being a consultant, you can influence change because you are brought in for your talent and for what you can contribute to the project.

Obstacles of Working as a Consultant

An issue you may face as a consultant on a learning experience is having a limited perspective on the entire project. I once did some consulting work for a bank, and I remember having to get two levels of approvals just for access to the branding documents. Organizations can be extremely protective of their intellectual property, despite having consultants sign non-disclosure agreements (NDAs). Sometimes, you are treated as an employee with access to everything you need, but other times it can be tedious to get the information necessary to make the project work. I've been on consulting projects that stopped abruptly due to a change in leadership, and I've had projects blossom into long-term working relationships. It can vary depending on the perspectives and information that you have access to.

Ways to Incorporate LXD in Consulting

Being a consultant on a project can be exciting, but it can also be difficult. If you are looking to bring in elements of learning experience design to a project, I encourage you to embrace your perspective as an outsider and to keep a list of recommendations. Not only will this list potentially help the organization if they decide to implement your recommendations, but it also can be a running list for you, as you grow and develop your own learning experience design process. I've documented some ways to incorporate learning experience design in your consulting work in Table 11-3.

Table 11-3. Ways to Incorporate Learning Experience Design in Consulting

Technique	Application
Embrace your perspective.	You likely don't have historical information about why an organization follows a certain process. As someone hired for your expertise, your voice potentially carries more weight. Use it to ask questions.
Keep a list of recommendations.	If you are unable to change processes or minds, and training courses are created that aren't optimal, keep a list of recommendations. Share these with your deliverable if it's a project-based contract; if you are on a long-term contract, share your recommendations with your leadership. Things may not change instantly, but keeping a record can help make the case for it.

Conclusion

Now that you have some additional background information about each setting and the different challenges, consider your current setting. How are my descriptions similar to or different from what you are currently facing? Reflect on what the benefits and obstacles may be in your environment as you incorporate elements of learning experience design into your practice. My hope is that you expand your horizons and continue to keep the user and performance in the center of what you create. In the next chapter, I will explore what it means to be an LXD champion.

30/60/90 Plan

As you look to incorporate pieces of this process in your own work, consider this 30/60/90 plan. The best 30/60/90 plans are made by you and are specific to your own situation. This one is a general template to get you thinking about how you can apply this strategy to your work.

30 days: Consider your current environment or where you want to work. What are the benefits and opportunities?

60 days: Select an opportunity to improve on or a benefit to continue taking advantage of. How is it affecting the learning experience?

90 days: Iterate and reflect on what has worked and what hasn't.

Conclusion
Becoming an LXD Champion

I'm going to end with a simple question: Would you want to take your own learning experiences?

Being vulnerable here, I would probably say no to this question more times than I'd say yes. I share this to let you know that things won't change overnight, and if you decide to adopt anything from this book, it will likely take time to implement. This book is full of words and ideas, but none of it matters if you can't apply them to becoming a learning experience design champion. There are four key traits of a learning experience design champion.

1. You create learning experiences that are anchored in the work (tasks) that someone needs to do to be successful in their job.

Creating learning experiences isn't about making stakeholders happy; it's about enabling people to do their jobs better. To do this, you need to understand what someone needs to do their job and how they do it. You can learn this by conducting a task analysis and documenting what they need to perform their job well. You also need to seek alignment on what success looks like—and having someone say that they "know" isn't enough, which leads to the second key trait of an LXD champion.

2. You don't assume that if a stakeholder says there is a training issue, it means you should automatically create a training solution.

You aren't in the discipline business. You aren't in the communications business. You are in the people business. While discipline and communication often intersect with your work, learning experiences shouldn't be used as punishments or communications. There are far more effective ways to do both. Before agreeing to anything, gather information about the problem people are trying to solve and why they think it is a problem. Often, these questions go unasked, and it's within the scope of your due diligence to ask them.

3. You create assessments that allow users to practice and apply the content to their work.

Assessments, when done correctly, are not only a way to provide users practice opportunities but also a way to measure what opportunities and successes people have on an individual level. This is also a nice way to provide an emotional hook by putting learners in realistic work-based scenarios that allow them to apply the content back to their jobs.

4. You are equally committed to learning and growing your own capabilities.

Commit to being a lifelong learner yourself. If you picked up this book, you likely already know you want to learn and grow. Don't rest on your laurels. Duration of time does not equate to mastery. Just because you have 20 years of experience doesn't necessarily mean you have more expertise than someone with three years of experience. Consider the LXD capabilities I've shared to determine which areas you can work on. I recommend selecting a level and a topic and either taking on stretch assignments at work to refine and grow your capability or talking with your team about learning as a group.

Stay curious and never forget the point of our work—to empower people and support them to do their jobs better. I'd love for you reach out to me to share your 30/60/90 plans or how you've been able to apply any of the ideas in this book to improve learning experiences in your organization. You can connect with me on LinkedIn at linkedin.com/in/caranorth11 and Twitter at @caranorth11.

References

Allen, M. 2020. "Mastering Techniques in Boredom." In "Components of Effective Learning," LinkedIn Learning, October 5. Video, 3:02. linkedin.com/learning/components-of-effective-learning/mastering -techniques-in-boredom?autoplay=true.

Bean, C. 2023. *The Accidental Instructional Designer: Learning Design for the Digital Age*, 2nd ed. Alexandria, VA: ASTD Press.

Clark, R.C. 2012. *Scenario-Based E-Learning: Evidence-Based Guidelines for Online Workforce Learning*. San Francisco, CA: Pfeiffer.

Clark, R.E., D.F. Feldon, J.J.G. van Merriënboer, K.A. Yates, and S. Early. 2007. "Cognitive Task Analysis." In *Handbook of Research on Educational Communications and Technology,* 3rd ed., edited by D. Jonassen, J.M. Spector, M.D. Merrill, J.J.G. van Merriënboer, and M.P. Driscoll, 577–593. New York: Routledge.

Couser, J. 2021. "Leading Creative Teams." Interview by J. Suarez and C. North. *Instructional ReDesign Podcast*. February 19. Audio, 37:19. instructionalredesign.com/2021/02/19/ep030-interview-with-jonathan -couser.

Dickelman, G.J. 1996. "Gershom's Law: Principles for the Design of Performance Support Systems Intended for Use by Human Beings." *CBT Solutions Magazine*, September/October.

Dirksen, J. 2015. *Design for How People Learn*. San Francisco, CA: New Riders.

Federal Communications Commission (FCC). 2021. "Closed Captioning on Television." Last modified January 27. fcc.gov/consumers/guides/ closed-captioning-television.

Hodges, C.B., S. Moore, B.B. Lockee, T. Trust, and M.A. Bond. 2020. "The Difference Between Emergency Remote Teaching and Online Learning." *EDUCAUSE Review,* March 27. er.educause.edu/articles/2020/3/the-difference-between-emergency-remote-teaching-and-online-learning.

Jordan, P.W. 2000. *Designing Pleasurable Products: An Introduction to the New Human Factors.* London: CRC Press.

Kirkpatrick, J.D., and W.K. Kirkpatrick. 2016. *Kirkpatrick's Four Levels of Training Evaluation.* Alexandria, VA: ATD Press.

Kuhlmann, T. 2009. "Build Branched E-Learning Scenarios in Three Simple Steps." *Rapid E-Learning Blog,* July 14. blogs.articulate.com/rapid-elearning/build-branched-e-learning-scenarios-in-three-simple-steps.

Merrill, M.D. 2002. "First Principles of Instruction." *Educational Technology Research and Development* 50(3): 43–59. doi.org/10.1007/BF02505024.

Moore, C. 2017. *Map It: The Hands-On Guide to Strategic Training Design.* United States: Montesa Press.

National Assembly of States Arts Agencies. n.d. nasaa-arts.org.

National Center on Accessible Materials. n.d. aem.cast.org.

Norman, D. 2013. *The Design of Everyday Things: Revised and Expanded Edition.* New York: Basic Books.

North, C., M. Shortt, M.A. Bowman, and B. Akinkuolie. 2021. "How Instructional Design Is Operationalized in Various Industries for Job-Seeking Learning Designers: Engaging the Talent Development Capability Model." *TechTrends* 65:713–730. doi.org/10.1007/s11528-021-00636-2.

PTI (Press Trust of India). 2018. "More Than 19,500 Mother Tongues Spoken in India: Census." *Indian Express,* July 1. indianexpress.com/article/india/more-than-19500-mother-tongues-spoken-in-india-census-5241056.

Quinn, C.N. 2021. *Learning Science for Instructional Designers: From Cognition to Application.* Alexandria, VA: ATD Press.

Thalheimer, W. 2022. *Performance-Focused Learner Surveys: Using Distinctive Questioning to Get Actionable Data and Guide Learning Effectiveness,* 2nd ed. Somerville, MA: Work-Learning Press.

Tillem, N. (@NickTillem). 2022. "Accessibility isn't extra steps, it's steps you've missed." Twitter, April 12, 2022, 9:46 a.m. twitter.com /NickTillem/status/1513876121250635790?s=20&t=wH0X05rOy -OpHRUwabPhXg.

Tofel-Grehl, C., and D.F. Feldon. 2013. "Cognitive Task Analysis-Based Training: A Meta-Analysis of Studies." *Journal of Cognitive Engineering and Decision Making* 7(3): 293–304. doi.org/10.1177/1555343412474821.

Usability.gov. n.d. "User Interface Design Basics." usability.gov/what-and -why/user-interface-design.html.

WebAIM. n.d. "Alternative Text." webaim.org/techniques/alttext.

World Wide Web Consortium Web Accessibility Initiative (W3C WAI). n.d. "Web Content Accessibility Guidelines (WCAG) 2 Overview." w3.org /WAI/standards-guidelines/wcag.

Xie, K., B.C. Heddy, and B.A. Greene. 2019. "Affordances of Using Mobile Technology to Support Experience-Sampling Method in Examining College Students' Engagement." *Computers & Education* 128:183–198. doi.org/10.1016/j.compedu.2018.09.020.

Index

Page numbers followed by *f* refer to figures.

About the Author

Cara North is an award-winning learning experience design leader who has 15 years of experience across many sectors of learning and development. Throughout her career, Cara has worked in various industries including e-commerce, higher education, manufacturing, healthcare, and consulting. Her leadership experience includes serving as operations training manager for a manufacturing facility in the semiconductor sector and as director of learning and development for a healthcare technology startup.

As a first-generation college graduate, Cara is committed to the empowerment and upward mobility of others through education and service. Cara holds a bachelor's degree in broadcast journalism from the University of Kentucky, a master of workforce development from The Ohio State University, and has completed all her doctoral coursework in learning technologies at Ohio State. She serves as an adjunct faculty member at several institutions, including Boise State, Eastern Kentucky University, and Boston College, teaching courses ranging from professional social media networking to program evaluation. Cara also formally served on the admissions committee for the master of instructional design and development program at the University of Alabama at Birmingham.

She believes in service to others. As a past chapter president of the Central Ohio Chapter of ATD (COATD), she started two programs, including the Emerging Professional Showcase to give new professionals an opportunity to gain speaking experience and COATD Loves Columbus to help members give to a local charity at networking events.

Outside of work, Cara's two main hobbies may not seem like they go together. You'll usually find her playing video games or attending a class at Orangetheory Fitness. Cara and her partner Mathew live in the Columbus, Ohio area with their cat Bib Fortuna.

About ATD

atd The Association for Talent Development (ATD) is the world's largest association dedicated to those who develop talent in organizations. Serving a global community of members, customers, and international business partners in more than 100 countries, ATD champions the importance of learning and training by setting standards for the talent development profession.

Our customers and members work in public and private organizations in every industry sector. Since ATD was founded in 1943, the talent development field has expanded significantly to meet the needs of global businesses and emerging industries. Through the Talent Development Capability Model, education courses, certifications and credentials, memberships, industry-leading events, research, and publications, we help talent development professionals build their personal, professional, and organizational capabilities to meet new business demands with maximum impact and effectiveness.

One of the cornerstones of ATD's intellectual foundation, ATD Press offers insightful and practical information on talent development, training, and professional growth. ATD Press publications are written by industry thought leaders and offer anyone who works with adult learners the best practices, academic theory, and guidance necessary to move the profession forward.

We invite you to join our community. Learn more at **td.org**.